Medicine's Brave New World

Medicine's Brave New World

Bioengineering and the New Genetics

Margaret O. Hyde
and John F. Setaro, M.D.

Twenty-First Century Books
Brookfield, Connecticut

Cover photograph courtesy of Roderick Chen/Superstock

Photographs courtesy of Photo Researchers, Inc.: pp. 14 (© Martin
Dohrn/IVF Unit, Cromwell Hospital/SPL, 107 (© Will & Deni McIntyre),
123 (© David Parker/SPL); AP/Wide World Photos: p. 16; TimePix: p. 35
(© Ted Thai); PhotoEdit, Inc.: p. 44 (© Mark Richards); Phototake: pp. 76
(© Roslin Institute), 105 (© Jean Claude Revy)

Library of Congress Cataloging-in-Publication Data
Hyde, Margaret O. (Margaret Oldroyd)
Medicine's brave new world / Margaret O. Hyde and John F. Setaro.
p. cm.
Includes bibliographical references and index.
ISBN 0-7613-1706-6 (lib. bdg.)
1. Medical technology—Juvenile literature. 2. Medical innovations—
Juvenile literature. 3. Medical ethics—Juvenile literature. 4. Medicine—
Forecasting—Juvenile literature. [1. Medical technology. 2. Medical
innovations. 3. Medical ethics.]
I. Setaro, John F. II. Title
R855.4.H833 2001
610—dc21   00-069083

Published by Twenty-First Century Books
A Division of The Millbrook Press, Inc.
2 Old New Milford Road
Brookfield, Connecticut 06804
www.millbrookpress.com

Contents

Chapter One
YOUR BRAVE NEW WORLD?

"I shall begin at the beginning," said the D.H.C. [Director of Hatcheries and Conditioning]…"These," he waved his hand, "are the incubators." And opening an insulated door he showed them racks upon racks of numbered test-tubes. "The week's supply of ova. Kept," he explained, "at blood heat; whereas the male gametes," and here he opened another door, "they have to be kept at thirty-five instead of thirty-seven"… he gave them…a brief description of the modern fertilizing process…how the fertilized ova went back to the incubators; where the Alphas and Betas remained until definitely bottled; while the Gammas, Deltas and Epsilons were brought out again, after only thirty-six hours….

—Aldous Huxley, *Brave New World*, 1932

In *Brave New World*, author Aldous Huxley portrays Earth in the twenty-fifth century as a planet where biologic engineering is used by an all-powerful benevolent dictatorship to ensure social stability and human happiness. The state regulates all

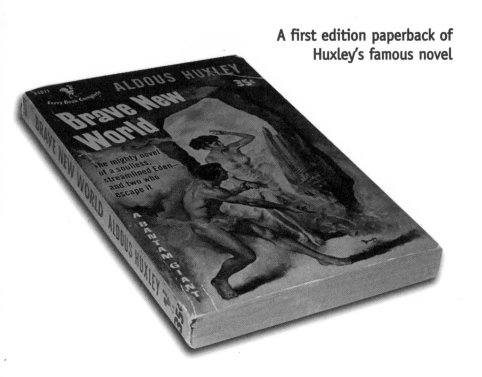

births, which are accomplished artificially, and creates classes
of human beings. Alphas, Betas, and Alpha Pluses are given the
best possible prenatal treatment and are programmed to be
directors. Other creatures are engineered to have a lower level
of intelligence, and their unskilled jobs as adults are defined
before they are born.

Throughout their childhood and adolescence people are
taught in their sleep, and they learn to give up truth and beauty
for ignorant bliss. Everyone is taught to be happy and have correct thoughts for his or her particular caste. People get what
they want and they never want what they cannot get. They are
never sick or afraid. But utopia comes with a price—creativity

is squashed and freedom is nonexistent. The people in this brave new world have never known true happiness; they know only happiness that is controlled and therefore false. Without sorrow, there is no true happiness. Religion, poetry, individuality, free thought, and free speech are unknown in this biologically perfect state-controlled paradise where all individuality and personal feelings are sacrificed for the sake of community.

People don't have the worries that people in our world have, but they don't know the joys either. If your best friend died, you would feel sad; in *Brave New World*, a person would feel just as happy as when the friend was alive. Huxley demonstrated the flaws of a controlled world where great sacrifices were made for a false happiness. Politically, he foresaw and warned against a government-controlled society in which people led dehumanized lives.

Today we are facing another kind of brave new world in which science and technology can shape the human condition. In sharp contrast to Huxley's prediction of a soulless, streamlined world in which emotions and ability are controlled by government, the new biotechnology is evolving swiftly in a climate of new personal freedom and decentralized control. Around the world, individual scientists, university and government laboratories, and biotech start-up companies are moving medicine ahead at an explosive rate.

Where will medicine's brave new world lead? Some of the technical developments in medicine and biology forecast by Huxley have already come to pass. Many aspects of reproduction can be regulated. Drugs, such as Prozac, can control moods. Surgery can remove parts of the body that don't work and, in some cases, replace them with ones that do. Animals can be cloned for the production of drugs that meet specific needs. Goats have been cloned to produce milk containing a protein that might be used to treat heart attack and stroke victims.[1] This is just the beginning of a field in which drugs can be matched to a person's genes, and other benefits may come. Other uses of cloning are more controversial. Already scientists are talking of cloning people. The promises and the perils of new advances in cloning make the need to separate fact from fiction one of the most important considerations for all citizens today.

Even deeper explorations into the very fabric of life are just over the horizon. With these discoveries will come an ability to manipulate the future of humanity in a way never before imagined.

Are we in a better situation than Huxley's fictional world? Will twenty-first-century citizens have the information and ability to decide what course the new biological revolution should take—who will benefit, what will be lost, what will be gained?

In this book, we cannot provide conclusions, but we will review current developments in order to frame the important questions. News of breakthroughs in the brave new world of medicine washes over the public in waves. Informed citizens must take part in the critical decisions to come. Knowledge about these issues will be crucial. Whether it is filled with hope or fear, the brave new world will be your world. You live on the cutting edge of a biological revolution.

ETHICS AND THE BRAVE NEW WORLD

Cloning, replacing genes, growing organs from single cells, replacing diseased or worn-out tissue with artificial tissue, and repairing damaged spinal cords are just a few of the many fronts that are being explored today. With these advances come many questions.

What will exploring life in laboratories do to the sanctity of life? The dignity of life can be open to different interpretations. Bryan Appleyard in his book *Brave New Worlds* asks if the dignity of the individual is better maintained by leaving his genome (genetic profile) alone or by pursuing research that might relieve his suffering or that of his children.[2]

How will commercial interests affect research? Many companies are now invited inside the halls of universities where complicated experiments require considerable financial support. Pharmaceutical companies are paying large sums of money to mine genetic databases.[3] Some companies are racing to identify and patent disease-causing genes to help in the production of new drugs. What will be the long-term social consequences of these partnerships? Will researchers and doctors always be wise?

You may soon carry your full genetic profile on a card in your wallet. In addition to helping to predict and prevent diseases, such a profile can help to determine the exact kind of medicine that is best for you. But your genetic profile card could be used to invade your privacy. Perhaps you would object to your profile being given to the government, insurance companies, your employer, or a prospective spouse.

No one expects the brave new world described by Aldous Huxley to come true, but as medicine moves into new territory, promises and dangers become everyone's concern. Is Huxley's nightmarish vision of future society a warning about possible things to come? While few scientists worry that the government might take over experiments in manipulating genes, many are concerned about what will happen if the government does not monitor new procedures and protect individual privacy.[4]

There will be grave decisions with no historical precedent. Young people of today will play a major role in the exciting new biology and medicine of the twenty-first century and in its moral and ethical implications.

BABY HAS THREE MOTHERS AND TWO FATHERS

FOR SALE: EGGS AND SPERM

WHERE IS THE TECHNOLOGY OF BABY MAKING
TAKING US?

For most couples who want children, making a baby is a private, romantic affair. But as these headlines indicate, for others it is a more complicated procedure.

About one in six couples in the United States cannot conceive naturally. In about a third of these cases the difficulty is traced to the woman, in another third to the man, and in the other third, both have problems.

When conception does not take place naturally, medicine offers a myriad of techniques to help those who

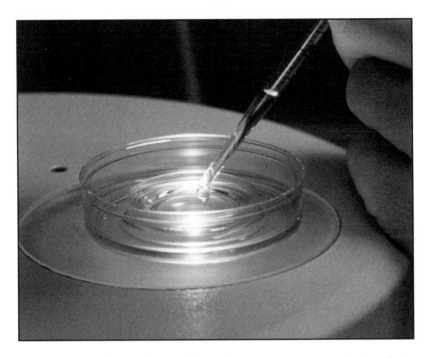

In vitro fertilization involves adding a father's sperm to a mother's egg in a plastic dish. This process can help infertile couples have children.

want a baby, including artificial insemination and in vitro fertilization. While the success rate for treating infertility can remain as low as 25 percent for each attempt, the many exciting new techniques in assisted reproduction are improving the chances. As techniques become more advanced, however, questions of ethics arise.

ARTIFICIAL INSEMINATION

Artificial insemination, the process by which a man's sperm is introduced by a syringe into a woman's vagina (birth canal), has been used to solve infertility problems for a long time, and it is widely used today.

Artificial insemination is often called for when the husband has a low sperm count. Normally, men have plenty of sperm to make women pregnant. Most men ejaculate anywhere from 40 million to 300 million sperm at a time. But in about one-third of the couples who cannot conceive naturally, the men produce less than 20 million and some less than 100. This makes pregnancy unlikely without high-tech help.[1] Using microsurgery, doctors have been able to retrieve sperm from the testicles of men who do not produce enough so they can become parents when the sperm is injected into the woman. Even if the sperm are weak and do not travel well, it takes just one sperm injected at the proper time to produce the beginning of a baby.

Artificial insemination is also used when men are impotent (can't achieve or maintain an erection) or sterile or carry genes for a serious disease. In the two latter cases, sperm donated from another man is used for the procedure. Most often the sperm is obtained from a sperm bank. This practice has been widely used for years, and huge numbers of donated sperm travel from sperm banks to clinics for use in artificial insemination each day.

When artificial insemination is not an option, doctor have other ways of helping infertile people have babies.

THE FIRST TEST-TUBE BABY

The birth of Louise Joy Brown on July 25, 1978, marked the beginning of an infertility revolution. Baby Louise was the first human conceived in vitro (outside her mother's uterus), a feat that followed ten years of research.[2] The baby's mother, Mrs. Brown, had been unable to conceive naturally because her fallopian tubes were blocked, and artificial insemination was not an option. While some thought this new way of making babies horrifying, others rejoiced.

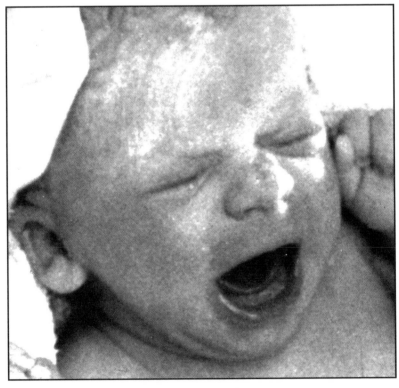

Baby Louise

The procedure for creating the first "test-tube baby" began with one of several eggs taken from the mother's ovary. Mrs. Brown had taken fertility drugs to stimulate her ovaries to produce several eggs. When the eggs were ready, she was sedated and an ultrasound probe was inserted through her vagina to locate the eggs. Then a large needle was passed up the vagina to retrieve them.

An egg was placed in a small plastic dish. Then sperm from the father were added to the droplet of culture fluid containing the egg, and fertilization took place. After the fertilized egg divided three times, it was placed in Mrs. Brown's uterus, where it developed into a healthy baby girl.

The procedure was painful, and the fertility drugs made Mrs. Brown uncomfortable in the days before it. Furthermore, she was told that stimulating her ovaries with hormones posed some risk. But she was more than willing to endure the pain and the risks to get her own child. Since that time, about 300,000 test-tube babies have been born around the globe using methods that involve in vitro fertilization (IVF).[3]

Today, eggs are retrieved for in vitro fertilization either by ultrasonic guidance, as described above, or by laparoscopic egg recovery, through a small incision in the abdomen. Eggs are placed in a special fluid medium; then semen that has been washed and incubated is placed with the eggs and left there for about eighteen hours. The eggs are removed and placed into a special growth medium, and about forty hours later, they are examined under a microscope. If the eggs have been fertilized and developed normally, several embryos are transferred to the woman's uterus. The probability of a pregnancy after one attempt is approximately 20 percent.[4]

DONOR EGGS

In situations where a woman's ovaries have failed or her eggs are not easily fertilized, eggs from a donor may be required. A woman in California in 1984 is believed to be the first to have given birth to a baby that began with a donor egg. Since then, between five and ten thousand babies have been born from donor eggs.[5]

But donor eggs are in very short supply. Not many women are willing to donate eggs. Why? First, the procedure for collecting eggs can be painful. Second, some potential donors worry about giving away their own genetic material. They feel that it is not right to give away a part of themselves that could lead to the birth of a child who would in many ways be like the donor but belong to another family.

Despite these problems, the use of donor eggs is becoming increasingly popular. It is one of the most common of assisted reproductive techniques.

Where are the eggs coming from? Some people get donor eggs from friends or relatives. Others receive eggs from women like Mrs. Brown, who had eggs left over from their own efforts to achieve pregnancy. In such cases, more eggs are collected than needed, and some of these women donate their unused eggs to infertile mothers. Still other eggs come from donors who are paid to produce them.

DONOR EGGS FROM FETAL TISSUE

Researchers are experimenting with a procedure that could produce an abundance of eggs to meet the needs of women on donor waiting lists. Fetal tissue, tissue taken from the ovaries of unborn fetuses, either aborted or miscarried, is a rich source of eggs.[6] A five-month-old fetus has cells that can produce seven million immature eggs.[7] A female baby is born with all the eggs she will ever have; immature eggs mature in the woman's body monthly. If immature eggs were removed from an aborted fetus and matured in the laboratory using microscopic techniques, large numbers of donor eggs would be available.

Another approach to solving the egg shortage would be to remove the eggs from aborted fetuses and store them in egg banks until they are needed. Then, when needed, they could be placed in a woman's body where they could mature and become part of her own reproductive cycle.[8]

Eggs Wanted

Egg Donor Needed. Financial Incentive.

Brianna is perplexed by this headline in her local newspaper. A childless couple is asking for a tall, intelligent, athletic, Ivy League college student to supply eggs for a procedure that will make it possible for them to have a baby. They are willing to pay $50,000 to the donor.

Brianna meets all the qualifications mentioned in the ad, and she needs money for tuition. Yet she feels selling her eggs is wrong, although she can't quite express why. After all, her body produces eggs every month that are of no use to her until she decides to have a baby. Why not help a childless couple? Would this be any worse than giving blood or selling hair, which many people do?

Although retrieving eggs from embryos and storing them in egg banks would help to solve the egg shortage, these procedures are quite controversial. People who consider abortion wrong are likely to consider the taking of fetal tissue from aborted fetuses immoral, whether the fetus was aborted naturally or deliberately. In addition, some worry about the long-term emotional effects of using fetal tissue or immature eggs on both the women who receive them and the woman who supply them. And what about the well-being of a child conceived this way? Would a child whose genetic mother was an aborted fetus be damaged in any way by learning this later in life? Using a fetus's ovary to generate life when the fetus itself was not allowed to develop may be the height of irony. The Ethics Committee of the American Society for Reproductive Medicine believes that the use of ovarian tissue from fetuses should not be pursued.[9]

ALTERING EGGS

A new procedure that could allow some infertile women whose tubes are blocked to have a child who is biologically their own involves altering an egg. First the nucleus of a healthy donor egg is removed and replaced by the nucleus of an egg from the would-be mother. This altered egg would then be fertilized with sperm from the father and implanted in the mother.

Some women resist being egg donors because they don't like the idea of giving away their own genetic material, but this technique would allow them to donate eggs safe in the knowledge that their own genes would not be used by another person. And the woman who received the altered egg could have the joy of knowing that her child carried her and her husband's own genes.[10]

SURROGATE MOTHERS

Surrogate mothers carry babies that have begun by in vitro fertilization from parents other than themselves. A surrogate may be willing to carry a child for a relative or close friend or even for a stranger.

The National Association of Surrogate Mothers is an organization that guides women who want to become surrogates. It helps with choosing an agency that will arrange the procedure and determining laws that relate to it. Many problems can arise with surrogate motherhood. Suppose the intended parents refuse to take the baby. Suppose the surrogate mother changes her mind and will not give up the baby. The association may be able to suggest a local support group for surrogate mothers.

DONOR SPERM INJECTIONS

A number of conditions cause infertility in men. When a man has a low sperm count, his sperm cells are often misshapen and cannot swim to fertilize an egg. When a man has a venereal disease or other infection, the tubes in which sperm mature may become blocked. Medicines and incomplete chromosomes can also cause infertility in men.

New techniques are helping here, too. In one procedure known as ICSI (intracytoplasmic sperm injection), sperm are harvested in the laboratory and injected into eggs that were kept in a proper medium in a petri dish after they were removed from the woman's body. Small glass pipettes, finer than the width of a human hair, attached to a micromanipulator are used to hold the egg and catch the sperm. In the more common procedure, in vitro fertilization, the sperm is not injected into the egg the way it is in ICSI. In both cases, the fertilized egg is then transferred to the woman. In both procedures, more than one egg is used to increase the chance of success.

DONOR EGG AND DONOR SPERM

Some couples require both donor eggs and donor sperm to achieve pregnancy.

Baby Samantha was born to an adoring couple, but she does not look like either of them. How come? Neither is her

23

biological parent. She was implanted as an embryo in her mother's uterus after she was created in vitro from a donor egg and donor sperm.

In rare cases, a baby may have three mothers and two fathers. Such was the case in California where a couple arranged to have a baby with donor sperm and donor egg implanted in a surrogate. Unfortunately, the couple was divorced before the baby was born and a legal battle over child support ensued. At one point, a judge ruled that the baby had no parents. Finally, it was determined that the couple who made the arrangement were the baby's legal parents.[11]

Critics of new reproductive technology point to this case and other controversies and contend that the "whole thing has gone too far." Where is medicine's brave new world taking us?

SAVING OVARIAN TISSUE

Doctors surgically returned some ovarian tissue to a dancer in 1999 after both her ovaries had been removed for medical reasons. Some of the tissue from one of her ovaries had been preserved by freezing before the surgery, and some of these egg-containing slices were later positioned in her body to act as an ovary and release eggs. The slices were positioned so that eggs could be released into her fallopian tubes and travel to her uterus as they would normally.

24

This ovarian tissue transplant technique appeared to work, so the technique holds hope for many women whose ovarian tissue is destroyed by radiation or chemotherapy.[12] It also holds hope for women who want to delay childbirth past menopause. But whether or not to extend a woman's childbearing years this way is highly controversial. How would an older mother fare with the burden of pregnancy? Would this mother be able to cope when the child was a teenager? Might she die before the child matured?

POSTHUMOUS REPRODUCTION

Suppose a woman, let's call her Hannah, was involved in a car crash shortly after she underwent an in vitro fertilization transplant. Her husband died in the crash and she miscarried the day after the funeral. Hannah desperately wanted to have her husband's baby. Luckily extra sperm from the in vitro fertilization remained frozen. Using the stored sperm for a new in vitro fertilization, Hannah was soon pregnant again with a baby who would be born about a year after the father was killed.

In Hannah's use of her dead husband's sperm there is little controversy. He meant for his sperm to be used to create their child. But suppose the husband died without leaving sperm behind? Would it be ethical to collect sperm from his dead body for the purpose of impregnating his surviving wife?

25

And suppose the man had said he did not want a baby? What then? Or suppose a woman is comatose and expected to die. Would it be ethical for her husband or his family to arrange to have eggs retrieved from her body and used with her husband's or a donor's sperm in a surrogate mother?

Doctors have been harvesting sperm from dead men for years. As far back as 1978, sperm was retrieved from a nineteen year old for the benefit of his parents, who wanted to continue their lineage.[13] But in many cases, families disagree about how the eggs or sperm of a deceased person should be used. Some people consider collecting sperm and eggs from dead people unethical. This and a variety of situations in which people disagree about harvesting sperm after death are among the many problems in medicine's brave new world.

FERTILITY DRUGS AND MULTIPLE BIRTHS

Taking fertility drugs is part of many procedures in assisted reproduction. These drugs stimulate the ovaries to produce eggs. In about one in ninety natural pregnancies, a woman produces more than one baby, but for women who have used fertility drugs the rate of multiple births is higher. Since the fertility drugs often cause a woman to produce many more eggs than her normal one at a time, this is not surprising.

With the increased use of fertility drugs, the number of multiple births involving three or more babies has tripled since 1980 and quadrupled since 1971.[14] And this is a problem. The average human uterus is designed to carry a baby of 6 to 9 pounds. When the uterus contains multiple babies, the total newborn weight of 6 to 9 pounds (2.71 to 4 kilograms) must be divided by the number of babies in the uterus. So the greater the number of babies, the smaller each will be. Babies who are small at birth tend not to do as well as babies of normal weight. In fact, the vast majority of multiple births of three or more end in disaster. Often the babies die or are severely impaired. Sometimes the mother dies or her health is affected.

When octuplets were born in Texas in December 1998, their birth reignited a long debate over what should be done to prevent multiple births and what can and should be done when they occur.[15] Although doctors who work with infertile patients are trying to avoid multiple births, more research is needed in this area.[16] Meanwhile, many doctors are dealing with the problem *after* conception. When it is discovered early in pregnancy that a mother is carrying a number of embryos, some doctors recommend that the development of some of them be stopped through a procedure called selective reduction—which is a fancy way of saying that some of the embryos are aborted. Reducing the number of embryos gives the remaining ones a better chance to reach a decent birth weight and survive. But this is not a very satisfactory solution, and some parents object to the procedure for religious, ethical, or emotional reasons.

CONFUSION AND CONTROVERSY

Couples who long for children point out that how children are treated and valued is more important than how they are conceived. Artificial insemination and the use of donor sperm and eggs are so common that they are no longer considered high tech, but the delicate issues surrounding many of these assisted reproduction procedures continue to be controversial. This is especially true when eggs are bought or sperm is chosen on the Internet, eliminating some of the medical guidance offered to prospective parents.

Many potential egg donors have questions about selling their eggs. They want to know what will become of the eggs that are donated. Will the parents ever tell the child that he or she has a biological mother somewhere? Many people feel it is not ethical to take money for something one's body produces. If you think it is ethical for parents to buy a donor's eggs for $5,000, do you feel it is wrong to offer $50,000? How much is too much?

Even before newspaper headlines like "Desperately Seeking Smart, Sensitive, Sunny Samaritan," questions arose about the ethical, medical, and psychological ramifications of egg donation. With the rising fees that are being offered, some ethicists and other citizens wonder if the donor procedure is getting out of control.

Even if prospective parents find the "perfect person for egg donation," no one can be sure of the genetic outcome. Suppose a baby that began with a $50,000 egg does not develop the qualities that were important to the parents. After all, tall women may harbor genes for shortness; brilliant women can bear retarded children. How might this affect the parents' feelings for the child? Might they refuse to accept the child? Might they sue if the baby doesn't turn out the way they wanted?

In the fall of 1999, the Ron's Angels Web site offered donor eggs from models to the highest bidder. There was no guarantee that the child that developed would be beautiful and fees might run over $100,000. Securing eggs through a Web site drew outrage from infertility groups and doctors, who complained that the auction was turning human eggs into a commodity. Trafficking in eggs is so distasteful to many people that the giant auction Web site, eBay, specifically banned auctioning eggs. They also refuse sperm, embryos, and other human body parts.[17]

Even where high-tech fertility procedures are accepted, battles continue over situations such as the use of frozen sperm after divorce, whether a woman has more control over an embryo than a man, and whether the embryos should be treated as people or property. Doctors everywhere are warning patients of the high cost of assisted reproductive techniques: medical, financial, and human. Social pressure against the millions of dollars spent to care for the premature babies that come with multiple births is increasing. But for many couples who have been trying to have a baby for years, no price seems too much.

Chapter Three
THE CHALLENGE OF SPINAL CORD REPAIR

Sarah never thought about her spinal cord until she had an accident. Later, the active fifteen year old learned how vital this 18-inch-long (46 centimeters) nerve fiber within her backbone is.

On the night of Sarah's accident, she had a few drinks at a friend's party. Then, as part of a game, she ran from a boy who was chasing her. While looking back to see if he was catching up to her, she dove into the friend's swimming pool. Normally, this would have been a cool thing to do, but the pool had been emptied for cleaning.

Vertebrae snapped as Sarah hit the bottom of the pool and some of the 20 million nerves bundled in her spinal column were crushed and twisted. Complex activity in nerve cells in Sarah's brain had allowed her to run without giving thought to how to run. Now, however, the messages that ran up and down her cord were interrupted.

Broken bones can be set. Skin can be grafted, and many other organs in the body can be replaced by transplants or artificial organs. But when the spinal cord is cut or crushed, a break of even a hair's width means silence between the nerve cells on one side and those on the other side of the injury. And this means paralysis. If she survived the accident, Sarah would be paralyzed from the neck down. She would no longer be able to use her arms or legs.

THE SECOND WAVE OF DAMAGE

Minutes after Sarah's spinal cord was compressed by the accident, a second wave of damage kicked off a kind of biological warfare.

Broken blood vessels caused small hemorrhages and the spinal cord swelled. Many cells starved to death when the normal action by which nutrients and oxygen are delivered to cells was stopped. Damaged cells spilled out a chemical called glutamate, which harmed neighboring cells. A series of destructive events took place including the production of free radicals, chemicals that damage living tissue.[1] Large numbers of nerve cells remained intact, but they became useless because they lost their insulating sheath, the layer of tissue called myelin. A fluid-filled cavity, known as a cyst, formed where the dead nerve cells used to be. This cavity formed a barrier to any nerve cells that might try to reconnect. Waves of cell suicide would continue to sweep through the area near the injury for days or weeks after the accident.

CONTAINING THE DAMAGE

People can function well with even a small number of neurons intact, so it is especially important to prevent or contain this damage. Within minutes after the accident, an ambulance rushed the unconscious Sarah to the local hospital, where an emergency team sprang into action. Immediately, this team administered MP (methylprednisone, a synthetic steroid). MP acts like a cease-fire agreement in the biological warfare that takes place in spinal cord injuries.[2] If the drug is given to a patient within eight hours of an injury, some of the damage appears to be contained. Other drugs are being investigated to promote survival of cells and limit secondary spinal cord damage, but this is the drug of choice now.

After being stabilized at the hospital, Sarah, still unconscious, was transferred by helicopter to a large hospital in the nearest city. When her parents reached her room, they begged for answers about her condition. The doctors' responses were guarded, for no one knew if Sarah would live or die. An operation called surgical decompression of the spinal cord was performed. This relieved any pressure from surrounding bone that could cause mechanical damage as well as cut off the supply of blood to the cells that remained alive.

RETRAINING THE SPINAL CORD

When Sarah regained consciousness, her shock was immense. She had been planning a modeling career. Now she had to face the fact that her dreams were dashed. She had always been fiercely independent, but now she had to depend on other people to wash her, feed her, dress her, get rid of bodily wastes, and tend to her every need. She found this humiliating. All she had to look forward to was regaining some of her independence. She yearned for the day that she could learn to move a wheelchair by puffing into a tube fastened in front of her mouth.

Sarah became one of the more than 200,000 people in the United States estimated to be spinal cord injured. On average, almost 14,000 cases of spinal cord injury are reported each year.[3] Of these, paraplegia, loss of movement and sensation in the lower body, affects 55 percent, and quadriplegia (loss of movement in both arms and legs) affects 44 percent.

Sarah often asked if the day would come when doctors would be able to repair her spinal cord so that she would have more control over her body. She spent hours thinking about Christopher Reeve, the actor best known for playing Superman, who became paralyzed after breaking the top two vertebrae in his neck in a riding accident. She had read Reeve's book, *Still Me*, and remembered some of the serious

As part of his physical therapy, Christopher Reeve uses a tilt table to help him adjust to a standing position in the hope of being able to walk one day.

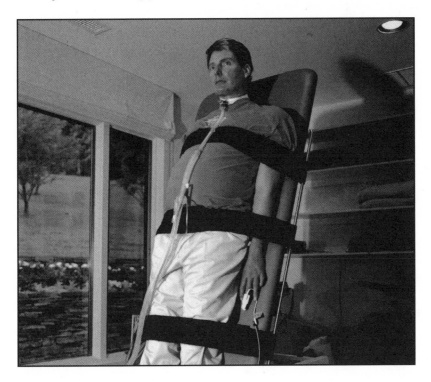

problems he bravely faced. She hoped he would continue to campaign for contributions to support exciting research by the many scientists around the world who are working to repair spinal cords. Reeve alerted the world to the needs of people who are paralyzed, people who have greater problems than most can imagine.

Is there any hope for patients like Sarah? Some. Recently scientists made an exciting discovery. Experiments showed that there is more flexibility and capacity for change throughout the spinal cord than they expected to find. In one experiment, forty-four people with spinal cord injuries were placed in harnesses that held them in place so they could be trained to walk on a treadmill. They practiced over a period of ten to twelve weeks. Before the experiment, only six could walk with walkers, and the rest were confined to wheelchairs. By the end of the program, thirty-eight could walk unassisted, using only canes or walkers. These patients had injuries in which the connection with the brain was not completely destroyed. This kind of treatment demonstrates that the spinal cord can be retrained and gives hope to many who have damaged spinal cords.[4]

WORKING TOWARD SPINAL CORD REPAIR

Spinal cord regeneration experiments are in their infancy, with much to be learned, but the progress already made gives hope to many of the hundreds of thousands of people in the United States who live with spinal cord injury. In the past there would have been no chance of improving the condition of those with spinal cord injuries. Growing new nerve cells was long thought to be impossible. But now doctors know better.

It still appears unlikely that there will be a single magic solution for repairing the spinal cord. Today, scientists in many parts of the world are working toward repairing spinal cords. Dr. Geoff Raisman in London and Dr. Jerry Silver in Cleveland along with their teams have been working on spinal cord repair for many years. They have proved that nerve fibers can be encouraged to grow through "white matter tracts" in the spinal cord. Cell bodies in the cord are in a butterfly-shaped core with nerve fibers extending out from the core. These spinal nerves branch out from the spinal cord and communicate with specific areas of the body. The nerve cells are wrapped in myelin, a white insulating material mentioned earlier. Getting the nerve cells to grow is difficult and complicated, but scientists have had some success.

In Stockholm, Sweden, Lars Olsen and other researchers succeeded in building a "bridge" across a tiny gap in the spinal cords of rats. They experimented with the repair of the spinal cords of some rats using a combination of grafts of neural tissue from outside the spinal cord and the addition of chemical factors for nourishment. Some axons of spinal cords that had been cut regrew. A number of rats that received the combination treatment immediately after their spinal cords were severed regained some ability to move their hind limbs and support body weight. None, however, regained the ability to walk.[5]

Researchers found that the axons of damaged cords do not grow back completely because chemicals in the area inhibit

SPINA BIFIDA

Spina bifida, a condition in which the tube that is to become the spinal cord does not close completely, is the most frequently occurring permanent disabling birth defect and, in some cases, one of the most devastating. It occurs in one of every thousand babies born in the United States. In many cases there are no symptoms even after the baby is born. In other cases, severe birth defects occur. There may be mental retardation, clubfeet, paralysis, and problems with urinating and controlling bowels.

When the discovery of spina bifida is made before birth, fetal surgery may make the difference between a retarded child in a wheelchair and one who is nearly normal. Although it is an operation with serious risks to mother and child, there have been many successful results.

To treat spina bifida in an unborn child, the surgeon makes an incision in the mother's abdomen, partially removes the mother's uterus, and places it on her belly. Then an incision is made in the uterus and

THE FETUS IS PULLED THROUGH IT. THE DOCTORS LOCATE THE FETUS'S SPINAL CORD AND USE SKIN AND MUSCLE TO CLOSE THE GAP OVER IT. THEY THEN RETURN THE FETUS TO THE UTERUS AND THE UTERUS TO ITS PROPER PLACE IN THE MOTHER. THERE THE FETUS CONTINUES TO DEVELOP UNTIL THE MOTHER GIVES BIRTH.

ABOUT 90 PERCENT OF CHILDREN BORN WITH SPINA BIFIDA NEED A SHUNT TO DRAIN EXCESS SPINAL FLUID. ONLY ABOUT HALF OF THE BABIES WHO UNDERGO THE FETAL SURGERY NEED A SHUNT. THEY ARE DELIVERED PREMATURELY, BUT MOST DO NOT HAVE PARALYSIS AND OTHER SERIOUS COMPLICATIONS AFTER THEY ARE BORN.[6]

SPINAL CLOSURE NORMALLY TAKES PLACE DURING THE FIRST MONTH OF PREGNANCY.[7] SCIENTISTS HAVE DISCOVERED THAT SPINA BIFIDA IS OFTEN CAUSED BY A MILD VITAMIN DEFICIENCY DURING THIS PERIOD. IF WOMEN TOOK 0.4 MILLIGRAM OF FOLIC ACID (ONE OF THE VITAMIN B COMPLEX) PER DAY BEFORE BECOMING PREGNANT AND DURING THE FIRST TRIMESTER, THE INCIDENCE OF SPINA BIFIDA COULD BE REDUCED BY 50 TO 75 PERCENT.

growth. Scientists are working to counteract these chemicals so that axons can grow. Then the axons must be trained to make the appropriate connections to the cells to which they were originally wired so they can function properly.[8] Much more needs to be learned before such experimental work can be tested on humans. For example, scientists must be certain that regrowing fibers can be kept under control once they have been triggered.[9]

A third exciting development involves a protein produced by a gene known as Nogo. Early in 2000, this gene was identified by teams of scientists in England and the United States. Nogo is present in the brain and spinal cord but not in other cells of the body. It appears that one of its effects is to prevent spinal cord cells from rewiring themselves after injury, for experiments in rats show that when the protein is blocked, the spinal cord can repair itself.

Since the interaction between Nogo and its receptor is known to prevent regeneration of axons after injury, the announcement in February 2001 by Dr. Stephen M. Strittmatter and colleagues at Yale University that they had identified the receptor was an important step in the goal of spinal cord repair. Now, Yale investigators are trying to find agents that block the binding of Nogo with its receptor.

A team of scientists at the Brain Research Institute in Zurich, Switzerland, have been working on Nogo for fifteen years but they have not yet identified the gene. Nevertheless, this team has created an antibody that blocks Nogo in animal experiments. Rats who were exposed to the antibody regrew several hundred nerve connections. Christopher Reeve hopes to take part in human tests after scientists learn more about the research.[10]

HOPE FOR THE FUTURE

Although damaged spinal cords may not be repaired anytime soon, the progress that has been made over the past decade dwarfs the progress made during all human history before that. Certainly, there is hope in the brave new world of medicine ahead that many who are paralyzed because of injured spinal cords will walk again.[11] Dr. Stephen Waxman, Yale University neurologist, believes that the goal of repairing spinal cords in the next decade, at least in some patients, is a realistic one.

GOING TOO FAR?

Not many people believe that Dr. Robert J. White's research with head transplants will become a reality—at least not in the near future. However, his experiments at Case Western Reserve University are not just scientific adventures. One of his goals is to help people who are paralyzed from the neck down. These people, for reasons that are not understood, often die prematurely from the failure of many organs.

According to Dr. White, it is not beyond science's reach to put someone's head on another body.[12] Transferring a paralyzed person's head to the body of a brain-dead person could prolong the paralyzed person's life. Although the idea of head transplants certainly seems like science fiction, some serious experiments are being done on animals, including monkeys. Many scientists think that human brain transplants are unlikely within the next twenty years because the nerve, blood vessel, and other connections that must be made number in the millions, making the procedure extremely complex. However, they refuse to say it is impossible in the distant future.

Even if a human brain transplant becomes possible, ethics committees may well find ways to prevent such a thing from happening. Consider how you would feel if a doctor asked you to give permission for the body of a loved one to be used in this way.

Chapter Four

SPARE PARTS FOR HUMAN BEINGS

Julian is seventeen years old. A virus has attacked and weakened his heart muscle so that it barely pumps. For three months, he has languished in the hospital's intensive care unit, requiring strong intravenous drugs and a surgically inserted device to keep his heart working. Many times he has come close to death. His only hope is that someday he will get a new heart.

With the coming of the summer vacation season, Julian indulges in a dark fantasy. The increased highway traffic means that there will be more accidents—a better chance that he'll get a donated heart from a brain-dead accident victim. Julian doesn't want to dwell on the fact that the victim might be a young person like himself who once had a promising future.

THE NEED FOR ORGANS

Julian is just one of thousands of patients who are waiting for new hearts or other organs. Where will these organs come

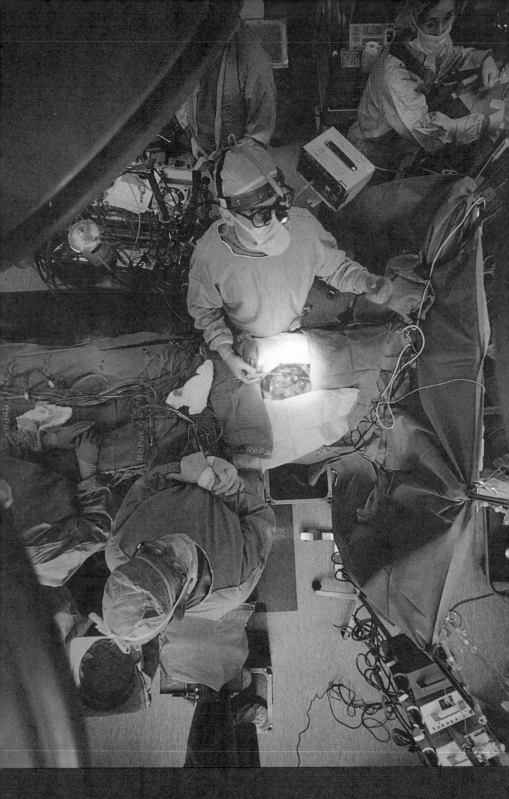

Surgeons use high-tech operating rooms such as this to perform
heart transplant and heart bypass surgery.

from? Unfortunately, most mechanical organs, such as the Jarvik-7 heart installed in Barney Clark in 1982, have not proved successful over time. So most patients today must wait for organs from donors.

Some patients like Julian are waiting to receive organs from accident victims. A few—for instance, those needing a kidney—may be able to obtain a healthy matching organ from a close relative willing to part with one. (People can survive with only one kidney.) But many will die before an organ is found.

Although modern medications make it possible to keep patients with failing hearts, kidneys, livers, lungs, and other organs alive for months on end, sooner or later they will die unless they receive an organ transplant. Yet despite donor organ programs and the public's awareness of the need for organ donations, donor organs are in short supply. In January 2001, almost 74,000 patients in the United States and many more worldwide were awaiting hearts, livers, or kidneys. Thousands of others with diabetes await pancreases. In the United States alone, 21,000 transplants take place annually, but almost 5,000 people die each year because organs for transplants are not available.[1]

Are there other solutions? Researchers think so. They are looking to new sources of replacement organs and tissue.

XENOTRANSPLANTS

Of all the bright promises of medicine's brave new twenty-first-century world, one of the most exciting is the prospect of using organs, parts of organs, or cells harvested from animals to replace worn-out or diseased human organs. This emerging field is called xenotransplantation, from the Greek word *xenos*, meaning "strange," "from a foreign species."

The main benefit of using animal organs, tissues, or cells is that they're more readily available than human parts. But, although there have been some successes, significant scientific barriers must be overcome.

First is the problem of rejection. The human body has a mechanism for rejecting foreign material, even when obtained from other human beings. The response is even more severe when the foreign organ or tissue is obtained from another species. The earliest and most devastating phase of this immune attack occurs when the recipient's body recognizes as foreign certain sugars on the cell surface of the donor organ. This inflammatory response is severe, destroying blood vessels in the transplanted organ. Later, there is an attack by other bodily defense systems. These assaults can be suppressed through the use of drugs that quiet the body's immune response. However, these drugs may also leave the patient

46

open to outside infections because they impair the body's ability to fight disease.

Second is the problem of disease. When tissue from an animal is transplanted into a human, there is the possibility that the recipient will become infected with a disease harbored by the animal from which the organ is taken. Is the risk of contracting diseases, known or not yet identified, from animal donors serious? Many scientists believe so. After all, a large number of viruses and other infectious agents can be transmitted from primates to humans. For instance, the Ebola virus and the human immunodeficiency virus (HIV/AIDS) are thought to have been transmitted to humans from primates in Africa long ago. Other animals pose a threat as well.

Mad cow disease (bovine spongiform encephalopathy), a dreadful disease that cows can get, leaves spongy holes in the brain and ultimately results in death. It appears to be caused by small biological particles, called prions, found in feed that contains by-products from infected cows. The latest tests reveal that the prion in mad cow disease matches the one in young humans who suffer from a new strain of a previously recognized disorder called Creutzfeldt-Jakob disease.[2] Since the prion matches the one in mad cow disease, it appears that people who eat meat from infected animals can develop the disease.

Even though pigs have been living at close quarters with humans for thousands of years without serving as a source of major human diseases, scientists worry about PERV (pig or porcine endogenous retrovirus), a virus commonly found in pigs that may have the potential to cause human disease. The HIV/AIDS virus is a member of the retrovirus family as well.

The great fear about xenotransplantation is that once a new virus gets into a person through an animal transplant, it could spread rapidly because the recipient's own immune system is being suppressed by antirejection drugs. This would endanger not only the person receiving the transplant, but also others. Theoretically, the disease could then be distributed throughout the defenseless human population by blood or sexual contact, or even perhaps through the air, as are respiratory cold viruses and tuberculosis. In that case, the benefit to the individual patient needing a transplant would be purchased at the cost of risking the health of society at large.

Obviously, xenotransplantation will not become a common or useful procedure until these obstacles are surmounted. As baboon bone marrow transplant recipient Jeff Getty pointed out at a meeting of the American Association for the Advancement of Science, safe sex practices will be a vital component in protecting society from xenotransplantation-related animal diseases.[3]

INITIAL ATTEMPTS

The first known attempt at xenotransplantation was performed in Russia in 1682, when a piece of bone from a dog was implanted into the skull of an injured nobleman. Initially successful, the operation had to be undone because of objections from religious authorities.

In the 1800s, the skin of frogs was used in attempts to heal burn victims. In 1905, a French surgeon implanted sections of rabbit kidney into a child who had kidney failure. The child's condition improved at first, but the child died several weeks later. Lamb kidney was tried in an equally fruitless effort in 1923.

In 1954 Dr. Joseph Murray performed the first successful human-to-human kidney transplant between identical twin brothers. His success inspired investigators to work in the field of animal-to-human transplantation. In 1964 a patient survived for nine months after receiving a chimpanzee's kidney.

In 1984 Dr. Leonard Lee Bailey implanted a baboon's heart into two-week-old Baby Fae, an infant who was born with a devastating heart defect. Baby Fae lived for only twenty days, and Dr. Bailey was criticized both for conducting the experiment and for not making a greater effort to find a human donor heart for the baby. But Bailey contended that donor hearts from infants are hard to come by and he couldn't wait for one. And at the time doctors were not sure whether an infant would mount a rejection response like a mature adult, and if so, whether the response would be fatal.

Less than a decade later, pioneering liver transplant surgeon Thomas Starzl transplanted baboon livers into two patients with terminal liver damage. The transplanted livers worked, but these patients ultimately died from infections. The strong medications used to suppress a rejection response weakened their ability to combat infections.

Since the mid-1990s, there have been promising developments in the quest to perform xenotransplantation of solid organs, such as heart, liver, or kidney. Survival times have improved in experimental operations transferring organs between pigs and primates, yet significant challenges remain before trial operations in human beings can be conducted.

DEALING WITH REJECTION

Rejection is always a possibility—even in human-to-human transplants. It becomes more acute when the transplantation occurs between different species. And the more distant the donor species, the greater the chance of rejection. For instance, humans are more likely to reject pig organs than they are the organs of more closely related primate species, such as baboons.

Scientists are attempting to meet rejection challenges in a number of ways. One way is to alter the recipient's own immune system in order to reduce the rejection response. Scientists have been working with baboons to see if injecting cells from pig bone marrow, the source of the body's immune defenses, will promote tolerance for a later pig organ transplant.[4]

Another way is to alter the genetic makeup of the donor animal so the recipient's body does not recognize the transplant as foreign and to give drugs to suppress any immune reactions. In an effort to make pig organs more like human organs and therefore more acceptable to the recipient's body, several research groups are developing transgenic animals. "Transgenic" means carrying genes from more than one species.

Since ancient times, humans have fantasized about combining species. Examples include the centaur, half man, half horse, and the Chimera, a blend of snake, goat, and lion. The first true transgenic creatures to contain human genes were mice, first bred in 1980 and now used frequently in cancer research.[5]

How can you alter the genetic makeup of an animal? By injecting human DNA (deoxyribonucleic acid), the chemical that contains genes, into the fertilized egg from which the animal develops. The procedure doesn't always work, however. In only a small minority of the animals produced in this manner does human DNA appear.

In some experiments, transgenic pig organs have been transplanted into baboons, who survived up to ninety-nine days, but human trials probably will not be conducted until scientists can prove much longer survival times.[6]

DEALING WITH INFECTIOUS RISKS

To limit the chance of passing diseases through xenotransplants, researchers keep experimental donor animals under extremely clean conditions so that they will not become infected with typical animal diseases. Pure water, air, and food are provided, and the animals are fed only plant or vegetable matter so as to avoid meat-borne prion diseases. Their pedigrees, or family histories, are carefully checked for illnesses, and they are tested for all known infectious diseases before organ harvest can be considered.

Yet researchers acknowledge that it may be difficult to eliminate completely the transmission of an unknown

TEMPORARY MEASURES

IN 1997 A YOUNG MAN IN TEXAS NAMED ROBERT PENNINGTON DEVELOPED LIVER FAILURE AND WAS NEAR DEATH. A DONOR ORGAN COULD NOT BE FOUND. SO DOCTORS HOOKED UP HIS CIRCULATORY SYSTEM TO THE LIVER OF A GENETICALLY ALTERED PIG, ONE BRED WITH HUMAN GENES FOR XENOTRANS- PLANTATION PURPOSES. THE PROCEDURE WORKED FOR SIX AND A HALF HOURS—LONG ENOUGH TO KEEP THE PATIENT ALIVE UNTIL A DONOR ORGAN COULD BE FOUND. THE PATIENT IS ALIVE AND DOING WELL TODAY. IN THIS CASE, A GENETICALLY MODIFIED ANIMAL ORGAN WAS USED AS A BRIDGE TO A MORE PERMANENT HUMAN-TO-HUMAN TRANSPLANTATION.[7]

microbe. As with HIV/AIDS, some types of animal infection may not produce illness in humans until many years after transmission. Diseases that are mild in animals might produce devastating sicknesses in humans. Some diseases could change into a more virulent form once introduced from animals into people.

Recognizing these concerns, the U.S. government proposed that, in addition to the safeguards listed above, researchers should preserve blood and tissue samples from all animal donors and human recipients. In this way, if new diseases or epidemics appear, their source and identity will be easier to track, and a link to xenotransplantation will be simpler to prove.[8] This information could be of value for future studies.

Recently, Novartis, a European pharmaceutical company, and the U.S. Centers for Disease Control and Prevention published reassuring information regarding infectious risks. Investigators looked at 160 patients who had been exposed to pig cells up to twelve years earlier and found no evidence of PERV infection.[9] This report led to optimism among xenotransplantation researchers. However, the possibility of PERV infection or disease due to another mysterious virus still remains.[10]

TISSUE TRANSPLANTS

Despite the problems of rejection and infection, the practice of xenotransplantation remains promising. "Even more promising," according to Dr. Leonard Bell of Alexion Pharmaceuticals, "is the prospect of replacing groups of individual cells in cases where disease or dysfunction arises from a small focus, or center of attention, of sick, dying, injured, or absent cells. Examples [of such cases] include spinal cord injury (200,000 patients in the United States), Parkinson's disease, a disease of the central nervous system (1,000,000 individuals), and congestive heart failure (nearly 5,000,000 in the United States alone)."[11]

The Alexion group has developed transgenic animals whose cells and tissues have greatly reduced levels of the cell-surface sugars generally recognized as foreign by the human body's response system. In addition, these animals have a protein that inhibits some of the rejection response. Thus cells and tissues from these animals have a good chance of being accepted by human recipients.

Dr. Bell's group has not yet transplanted these cells and tissues into humans, but experiments with human blood have shown that such cells are protected from destruction when exposed to human blood and that transgenic pig organ transplants have favorable results in primates. In 1998 Dr. Bell's group transplanted transgenic pig nerve cells into other animals that get Parkinson's disease or have spinal cord injury, with good recovery of normal nerve function in both experiments.[12]

The prospect of using tissue transplants to treat Parkinson's disease and other disorders of the central nervous system is particularly exciting. In Parkinson's disease, the brain does not manufacture enough dopamine, a vital chemical messenger that allows nerve cells to communicate. As a result, the section of the brain that controls muscle function is compromised and the muscles become so rigid that the patient cannot walk nor perform simple activities such as brushing their teeth, writing, or even feeding themselves. Powers of speech also deteriorate sharply. Some patients have been successfully treated with drugs, but for others drugs were either unhelpful or not tolerated in doses adequate to do any good. For these patients, tissue transplants may be an answer.

Already Dr. James Schumacher, a brain surgeon at the Lahey Clinic, outside of Boston, led one study that aroused particular interest. His group transplanted fetal pig cells into the brains of Parkinson's disease sufferers and reported at least some improvement in all patients. Certain participants experienced relief from tremors and rigid muscle symptoms for as long as two years after the operation.[13] An ongoing study is evaluating similar pig tissue transplants in patients with Huntington's disease, a severe hereditary central nervous system derangement.

The early experience with cell or tissue transplantation from animals to humans has been somewhat encouraging. As mentioned earlier, in 1995 AIDS patient Jeff Getty received a transplant of bone marrow cells from a baboon in the hopes that the transplant would boost his immune system and help him resist HIV. (Baboons are HIV-resistant.) Getty tolerated the bone marrow xenotransplantation well and is alive today. In other trials, adrenal gland cells from a fetal calf have been inserted near the spinal cord to relieve pain in human cancer patients, and diabetic patients have received implants of pig pancreas cells to spur their systems to produce insulin of their own.

TISSUE ENGINEERING

The time: ten years in the future. Through tissue engineering, scientists have developed a way of creating new organs out of plastic and human tissue.

Josh, a diabetic, is one of the first recipients of this new procedure and he couldn't be happier. Josh remembers the bad old days before he got what he calls his plastic pancreas. Since early childhood, he needed multiple daily needle injections of insulin to treat his diabetes. He recalls the many medical crises when he was rushed to the hospital because his blood sugar level dropped too low or rose dangerously high. Even harder was his constant struggle to live a normal life while friends pursued athletic, travel, and social interests that he wished he could join but that were impossible for him. Now that Josh has a new pancreas, he no longer has to worry about his blood sugar levels all the time. It is hard to share his joy, however, because no one else even remembers that Josh was once a diabetic.

The brave new world of tissue engineering began with the use of skin grafts grown outside the body for use in burn victims. Will medical science ever be able to grow three-dimensional tissue structures or organs outside the body for use when natural parts or organs fail? Scientists think so.

Exciting medical and engineering approaches are being used to grow new tissues, including pancreas, liver, kidney, bone, teeth, urinary bladder, spinal cord, cornea, cartilage, intestine, heart, breast, and arteries. In one example, cells are grown in a three-dimensional structure made of biodegradable polymers, like the materials from which dissolving surgical stitches are made. When transplanted, the polymers vanish, leaving a functioning organ constructed purely of living cells.[14] The original cells may have come from a donor or from the patient who needs the transplant. This method is particularly useful in creating new bone when fractures will not heal. The engineering of cartilage, which needs little nourishment and requires no new blood vessels, will prove helpful in the 500,000 operations done each year in the United States to repair damaged joints. New cartilage would also be a welcome addition to another nearly 30,000 surgeries in which inborn or traumatic head and facial deformities are corrected.[15]

Recently, a heart valve was grown in a bioreactor using sheep cells seeded onto biodegradable scaffolding, and then the valve was successfully implanted into an animal where it functioned normally.[16] According to advocates, if tissue engineering becomes a reality, then scarce organ donations, infection, rejection, and the need for drugs to suppress the immune system would no longer pose problems.

Considerable challenges remain, however. Where will the new blood vessels that are needed to feed the new organs come from? Research is under way to refine biochemical substances that promote blood vessel growth. In an area pioneered by Dr. Judah Folkman, a surgeon at Boston Children's Hospital, these substances were first identified by studying cancers that grow their own blood supply. Angiogenesis, or the creation of new blood vessels, is a method that will play a major role in the tissue engineering of larger organs. But more work needs to be done to identify the natural substances that promote liver growth, for example. Nonetheless, many experts confidently predict that tissue engineering will become a major pillar of twenty-first-century medical treatment.

ETHICAL ISSUES: HOW FAR IS TOO FAR?

As science makes advances in the fields of xenotransplantation and tissue engineering, many questions arise. One area of concern is the potential health risk of receiving animal organ transplants. Another is the ethics of using animals to supply human organs, and a third is concern that the melding of human and animal life forms may have disastrous results.

The possible transmission of infectious diseases between species is always an issue. Both AIDS and Ebola, which have been thought to have jumped from another species to humans, are deadly diseases. No one knows exactly what could happen if transplants from other animals became common practice, but there is fear of the transmission of new diseases that could not be contained.

Some people question the ethics of using animals as xenotransplantation donors. Animal rights activists are particularly concerned about using endangered species like chimpanzees and other primates. And while there are fewer ethical objections to using pigs, since they are routinely raised for food in large numbers anyway, questions as to whether the life of any animal should be sacrificed to save a human being have been hotly debated.[17]

In the new biological and transplant sciences, is there a line that everyone agrees should not be crossed? Is an experiment possibly leading to the birth of a child that is part cow and part human going too far?

On November 14, 1998, President Bill Clinton wrote the following to Dr. Harold Shapiro, president of Princeton University and head of the National Bioethics Advisory Commission:

This week's report of the creation of an embryonic stem cell that is part human part cow raises the most serious of ethical, medical, and legal concerns. I am deeply troubled by this news of experiments involving the mingling of human and non-human species.[18]

The event provoking the presidential letter was a revelation that scientists at a small biotechnology company, Advanced Cell Technology, had implanted a nucleus containing human DNA into a cow's egg that had been emptied of its own DNA. One of the researchers had obtained the human DNA from cells lining the inside of his own mouth. He thus avoided the need for permission to experiment on human subjects, since there has never been a rule against experimenting on oneself.[19] Of major interest, the cell reverted to its embryonic state, meaning that with the correct stimulation it could eventually become something else—perhaps a specific type of transplantable tissue, organ, or even a living being.

The advantages of creating human cells this way are clear. Cow eggs are freely available, and human DNA is easy to retrieve from the mouth or from blood samples. So, without using ethically controversial human fetal cells, embryos, or cloning techniques, an individual could have spare parts manufactured using his or her own genetic blueprints. But could the same technique be used to develop a monster-child, half cow, half human?

The Bioethics Commission concluded that, based on available evidence, a pregnancy using a hybrid egg cannot be maintained under the current state of knowledge. Nevertheless, it declared, an attempt to develop a child from such cells should not be permitted.[20] But research will continue, under the stated ethical guidelines, in the use of cow eggs to get human cells in shape for possible tissue or organ transplantation.[21]

Chapter Five

EXCITEMENT ABOUT STEM CELLS

The awesome potential of stem cells is a recent discovery that has created great excitement in the world of medicine. Think of a stem cell as a kind of master cell. Some stem cells divide over and over and give rise to the human being. They can give rise to the 210 kinds of cells in the human body. Scientists are moving toward the day when they can inject special kinds of stem cells into a variety of human organs, where they will replace diseased and dying tissue. Stem cells hold great promise for treating a myriad of human ailments, including Parkinson's and Alzheimer's diseases, spinal cord injury, stroke, burns, heart disease, diabetes, osteoarthritis, and rheumatoid arthritis.[1]

A NEW FRONTIER

The hoped-for day grew closer after two groups of scientists announced on November 6, 1998, that they had isolated, identified, and cultured human stem cells. The stem cells were capable of forming the tissues that give rise to distinct human

GROWING STEM CELLS

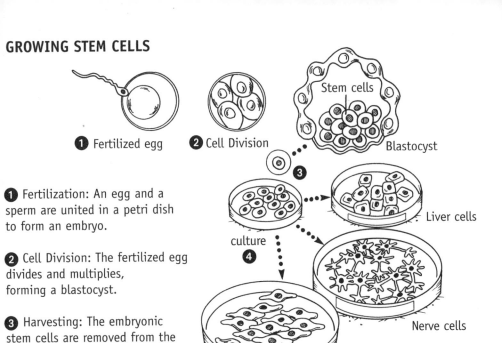

1 Fertilized egg   **2** Cell Division   Stem cells   Blastocyst

1 Fertilization: An egg and a sperm are united in a petri dish to form an embryo.

2 Cell Division: The fertilized egg divides and multiplies, forming a blastocyst.

3 Harvesting: The embryonic stem cells are removed from the blastocyst. (The embryo can no longer survive to become a fetus.)

4 Specialization: The stem cells are placed in cultures, where they will multiply and begin to differentiate into specialized cells.

culture

Liver cells

Nerve cells

Muscle cells

cells such as muscle, heart, bone, and nerve. This important scientific breakthrough brought biomedical research to the edge of a new frontier.

One group of researchers, headed by Dr. James A. Thomson of the University of Wisconsin, isolated embryonic stem cells in the stage before an embryo was formed. After an egg is fertilized, it divides several times and forms a hollow sphere, known as a blastocyst. A blob of fifteen to twenty cells piles up, forming an inner cell mass against a wall of the blastocyst. Dr. Thomson and his colleagues cultured embryonic stem cells from this mass of cells, using blastocysts that were left over from in vitro fertilization.[2]

Dr. John D. Gearhart of Johns Hopkins University worked with nonliving embryos from terminated pregnancies. (Informed consent was obtained from the donors after they had independently decided to terminate their pregnancies.) Dr. Gearhart took stem cells from the region of the fetus that was destined to develop into the testes or the ovaries.[3] This embryonic tissue was placed in a carefully selected nutrient and growth factor bath to develop into true stem cells.

Since embryonic stem cells are capable of forming many kinds of tissues, their culture in the laboratory created enormous excitement among scientists. In addition to being used to cure diseases, research on human stem cells may provide new information in basic biology, foster the discovery of new drugs, aid the study of infertility and birth defects, and lead to the development of new therapies for transplants. There is almost no realm of medicine that might not be benefited.

Not all stem cells can produce different kinds of cells. As an embryo develops, embryonic stem cells mature and become committed to developing specific types, such as those that repair liver, blood, and other organs. Yet even these more specialized stem cells are being used in exciting new ways.

Stem Cell Primer

There are three basic types of stem cells.

Totipotent stem cell: The single cell, or agate, formed when an egg is fertilized by a sperm. This fertilized egg becomes the embryo and can form a complete individual.

Pluripotent stem cell: Totipotent cells develop into a hollow sphere known as a blastocyst approximately four days after the egg is fertilized. A cell mass of pluripotent stem cells forms inside the blastocyst. These pluripotent stem cells are capable of forming virtually every kind of cell found in the human body. They can be removed and grown in great numbers and they can be directed to form cells that, in turn, make various tissues of the body. They cannot form a human being because they are unable to give rise to a placenta and supporting tissues necessary for development in the human uterus.

Multipotent stem cell: This type of stem cell, which develops from pluripotent stem cells, is also known as an adult stem cell. Adult stem cells, which are found in children and adults, are more specialized than pluripotent stem cells. They give rise to cells that have specific functions. Some, for instance, give rise to red blood cells while others give rise to nerve, skin, or other cells. There is evidence that multipotent stem cells from adults may not have the same capacity to proliferate as those from children or from embryos.[4]

BLOOD STEM CELLS

The cells in your blood have a short life. The red cells last several months, the platelets that control bleeding last from a few days to two weeks, and many kinds of white cells last from a few days to a few weeks. The supply of these cells is continually replenished by blood stem cells like those that live in the bone marrow of every child and adult. A small number of blood stem cells can also be found circulating in the bloodstream. A transplant of blood stem cells can save lives.

A boy named Keone was the first person to receive a blood stem cell transplant for sickle-cell disease, a disease that causes great pain when odd-shaped blood cells get stuck in blood vessels. At the age of five, Keone had a stroke, one of the complications of sickle-cell disease. For the next seven years, he suffered continuous and excruciating pain in spite of monthly blood transfusions. Although some sickle-cell patients had been successfully treated with bone marrow transplants, doctors had been unable to find a close enough bone marrow match for Keone from a relative or the national donor registry.

Then, on December 11, 1998, when he was thirteen years old, Keone underwent an experimental procedure at Atlanta's Egleston Childrens Hospital of Emory University. After ten days of chemotherapy to destroy his own bone marrow that contained sickle cells, Keone received a transplant of blood taken from a newborn's umbilical cord. Umbilical cord blood, blood that remains in umbilical cords and placentas after babies are born, is rich in stem cells. These cells can grow new marrow.[5] The cord blood transplant gave Keone a whole new system of red cells, white cells, and platelets. It appeared to eliminate all traces of the disease, and after a year he was declared cured.[6]

This operation was groundbreaking on three fronts: the donor blood was not a complete match; the donor was not related to the patient; and this was the first time that a sickle-cell patient was treated with cord blood. Cord blood is currently being used to treat a number of other diseases, including leukemia, immune disorders, and anemia. Because of its great disease-fighting potential, a number of parents are banking cord blood when they have a baby in case it's needed later, but some experts in the field frown on this, saying that since the blood will probably never be needed it is foolish to spend the money to collect and store it.[7]

Walter was helped by stem cells in a different way. He was suffering from leukemia, a kind of cancer that involves white blood cells. Walter needed large doses of chemotherapy and radiation to treat his leukemia, so doctors removed stem cells from his blood before his disease progressed to the stage

69

where he needed harsh treatment. They froze the stem cells and returned them to his body after radiation and chemotherapy. Just a small number of stem cells were needed to repopulate his blood.

Doctors at Yale–New Haven Hospital have been performing stem cell transplants since 1993—as many as 150 a year. Although blood stem cell transplants are now fairly common in the United States, Canada, and Europe, few people had heard of stem cells until the exciting new discoveries in 1998 gave promise that all kinds of stem cells can be grown from embryonic tissue.

ADULT STEM CELLS

While adult stem cells have long been known to play a part in tissue healing in most organs of the body, doctors thought the adult brain was an exception. Now, experiments show that adult neural stem cells can redefine themselves, even forming blood cells. In fact, a single neural stem cell can change during cell division into any of the three major types of cells in the brain and spinal cord.[8]

Adult stem cells are the "new kids on the block," according to Dr. Roger Pedersen of the University of California at San Francisco. Work with mice showed that stem cells from the adult mouse brain can be coaxed to differentiate into liver, heart muscle, and other types of cells.[9]

Recently, Dr. Ronald D.G. McKay of the National Institute of Neurological Disorders and Stroke in Bethesda, Maryland, and other researchers discovered that stem cells from the central nervous system will divide in culture outside the body if given the proper nutrients. As a result, researchers now have large numbers of stem cells to study and experiment with. After much more is learned, neural stem cells may be used to treat Parkinson's disease, to repair parts of the brain lost to injury or disease, and to develop new ways of stopping the growth of cancerous brain tumors.

GROWING ORGANS

Every fourteen minutes, a new name is added to the national organ transplant waiting list.[10] Xenotransplants may someday help to supply organs, but researchers are also experimenting with ways to create new organs from stem cells. It is a complex process that may be a long way off.

A big step toward growing replacement parts for humans was taken by researchers at Osiris Therapeutics, a company in Baltimore. Researchers there isolated a single cell, called a mesenchymal stem cell, and grew it through more than twenty generations to become a colony of more than a million cells. Mesenchymal cells, which are produced in adults, give rise to bone, cartilage, tendon, muscle, and fat cells. The ability to grow mesenchymal stem cells in culture opens up the possibility of growing such tissues for replacement. Osiris Therapeutics is now developing products using mesenchymal stem cells from different human donors to regenerate bone in spinal fusions and long bone defects. The availability of bone regeneration products may revolutionize the practice of orthopedic medicine. Products may be available "off the shelf" to patients at the time of injury or surgical procedure.[11]

While research on stem cells is giving promise to many who suffer from diseases that have damaged vital organs, rigorous clinical testing must be done before patients benefit from it. Some researchers believe that organs will never be grown from stem cells, while others say that, in five to ten years, stem cells may be the basis of growing whole organs for transplant.[12]

STEM CELLS FOR THE HEART

Suppose it is forty years into the future and you have had a serious heart attack. You are taken to a large city hospital where doctors have been experimenting with stem cell transplants. You agree to undergo an experimental stem cell transplant that might save your life even though doctors warn that it is dangerous and may not help you.

After you are accepted for the new treatment, technicians take some skin cells from your arm and send them to the lab, where their genetic material is removed. Then, using the process known as nuclear transfer, the central technology of cloning, the nucleus is removed from some human eggs that have been discarded from in vitro fertilization procedures, and your genetic material is inserted into the eggs.

After a week of growing in the laboratory, early-stage embryos develop that contain genetic material from your skin cells. Technicians remove embryonic stem cells from these early-stage embryos and culture them to produce heart muscle stem cells. These are then transplanted into your heart. If these new cells grow and reproduce in your heart, they will replace some of the cells that died during your heart attack.

There are many hurdles, including some ethical concerns, before the above scenario moves from science fiction to fact, but new technologies may make it possible to use skin cells or other easily collected cells for tissue transplants.

A SLIPPERY BIOETHICAL SLOPE

The work being done with adult stem cells is generally accepted by most doctors and the public, but experimenting with and using embryonic stem cells continue to be controversial. Should scientists experiment with cells from which human life is created?

Embryos are now routinely created in clinics to help women who are having difficulty in becoming pregnant.

Generally, more are created than are needed, and most of the unused ones are destroyed. Others are donated to science. Unless they are implanted in a uterus, these cells have no ability to develop into a human being.[13] Nonetheless, for those who believe that human life begins at the time of conception, this use of embryonic cells in research is deeply disturbing.[14] They believe the dignity of these cells needs protection by law, and they argue that it is not possible to destroy a human embryo in an ethical manner. Others argue that collections of frozen embryonic cells the size of a dot, or even microscopic, need not be treated as human embryos.

Although research on embryonic stem cells was long permissible on privately funded projects, no federal funds could be used for this kind of research until the year 2000, when new federal guidelines were established. Congress had held debates on these new guidelines and invited the public to express opinions by contacting the National Institutes of Health (NIH).[15] Individuals were also invited to participate in discussions of the subject on the Internet.

After much discussion, the NIH revised the stem cell guidelines, and on August 23, 2000, the government announced that it would allow scientists to conduct federally funded research on human embryonic stem cells. While the bill allowed government funding for research on stem cells, it did not permit direct finance of the removal of cells from embryos. The cells could be obtained only from private researchers who extracted them from surplus embryos that would otherwise be destroyed by fertility clinics. Opponents criticized this separation as meaningless and wanted scientists to concentrate on research using only adult stem cells. A notice of correction of these guidelines was published in November 2000. And the debate continues. The latest information about stem cell research guidelines can be found on the NIH Web site, www.nih.gov.

Many medical researchers who are studying both embryonic and adult stem cells believe that both paths must be followed. Although some studies show that adult stem cells are more flexible than believed earlier, they do not have the same plasticity as embryonic stem cells. The quality of the adult stem cells is not as good as that of the embryonic stem cells and declines over time. Researchers say that it would be foolish to abandon embryonic stem cell research, which offers such great promise of relieving human misery.

On July 5, 1996, geneticist Dr. Ian Wilmut of Scotland announced that he had successfully cloned a lamb named Dolly from the cell of an adult sheep in a process called somatic cell nuclear transfer, or SCNT.

Dolly began with a cell from the mammary gland of a six-year-old ewe, Belinda. The researchers took an immature egg cell from another ewe and removed the genetic material

Dolly

from its nucleus. The egg cell without the nucleus provided the basis to support the genetic material from Belinda's mammary gland cell. Both cells were combined in a laboratory dish. Then a protein was added that caused the cells to fuse. The researchers gave the fused cell a tiny jolt of electricity to start the process of embryo growth. Next they implanted the tiny embryo in another sheep, a surrogate mother, who carried the embryo to term. When Dolly arrived, her cells underwent genetic tests to make certain she was definitely a clone of Belinda. She was.

The cloning of Dolly was the first successful cloning of a mammal. The cloning of other mammals followed—mice, goats, and calves. Monkeys have been cloned by splitting embryos, but this is different from cloning using an adult cell.

WHAT IS A CLONE?

We have seen how a clone was made. But what exactly is a clone?

In many ways a clone is similar to an identical twin. Identical twins are clones of each other. But identical twins begin after conception when a zygote, a totipotent stem cell, divides into two. The twins develop from these two embryos. A clone like Dolly, on the other hand, is the twin of its genetic parent.

Is a clone an exact replica of the original? Is it genetically identical? Physically, intellectually, and emotionally identical? If we look at twins, we can get some answers. We know that although identical twins look a great deal alike, they are not carbon copies of each other. There are slight variations in their features. And as they grow up, they develop

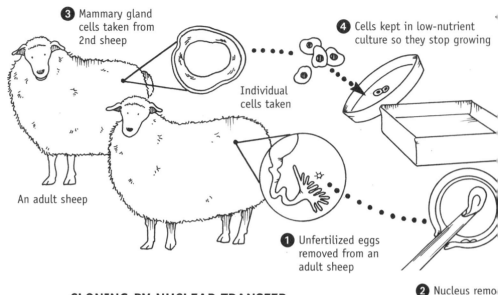

3 Mammary gland cells taken from 2nd sheep

4 Cells kept in low-nutrient culture so they stop growing

Individual cells taken

An adult sheep

1 Unfertilized eggs removed from an adult sheep

CLONING BY NUCLEAR TRANSFER

2 Nucleus remo from egg cell with tiny pip

Scientists learned how to clone sheep in 1996, and the first clone, Dolly, was born on July 5, 1996. How did they do it?

---

different personalities and their brains develop differently as well. Clones will show these same kinds of differences. The human brain is a complex organ. Although the genes indicate the rough layout of the wiring of the clone's brain, the brain makes and breaks many millions of connections as it develops that would make the clone different in many ways. He or she would always have a unique set of memories built on personal experiences and a unique consciousness. Environment plays a part in making twins—and clones—different, even though they have the same DNA.

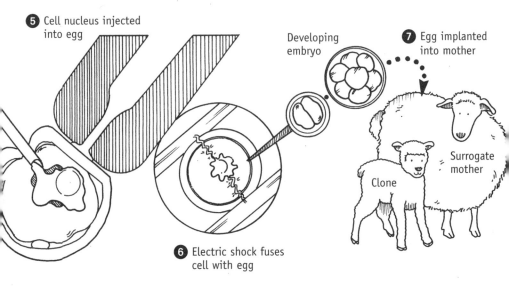

5 Cell nucleus injected into egg

6 Electric shock fuses cell with egg

Developing embryo

7 Egg implanted into mother

Surrogate mother

Clone

HOW LIKELY IS HUMAN CLONING?

The successful cloning of Dolly gave rise to many colorful and imaginative scenarios about the possibility of human cloning. In one example, three clones pretend to be a pair of twins so that they could carry out a crime by proving that the "twins" both had alibis. The third clone is able to commit the crime, since his existence is unknown. In another example, a parade of thousands of little Hitlers goose-stepping in rhythm take control of their country, generation after generation of clone after clone.

How likely is human cloning? Dr. Wilmut, Dolly's creator, thinks cloning people is unlikely. He points out that although scientists have plenty of animal eggs and cells with which to experiment and an abundant population of potential surrogate (animal) mothers, the success rate of cloning animals is not high.

In the case of Dolly, for instance, out of 277 attempts at fusing cells, only 29 of the fused cells became embryos, and these embryos resulted in only one pregnancy—the one that became Dolly.[1] Where would researchers get enough human eggs for such experiments? And if they had success in forming embryos, where would they get the surrogate mothers to bring them to term?[2] Besides, there are many other problems to overcome before human cloning should or could be considered.

In animal cloning there have been many disastrous outcomes. Many cloned animals have been born with hideous deformities and serious defects. Before human cloning is likely, scientists would need to make sure that the results would not be disastrous. No one expects Frankenstein monsters, but many are concerned about the possibility of cloned babies being born with terrible defects.

In addition, there are questions as to whether clones would have normal lifespans.[3] In May 1999, researchers found that certain structures in Dolly's cells, called telomeres, appeared slightly stunted, perhaps reflecting the age of Belinda, the sheep from which she was cloned. Telomeres are structures attached to chromosomes that get shorter each time a cell divides until it dies. Not only do telomeres prevent chromosomes from sticking together, they trigger a cell's inability to reproduce when they reach a certain length. Shortened telomeres may mean a shorter than normal life for a cloned animal.[4]

Other scientists disagree with these negative views of cloning. They believe that it is just a matter of time before the technical problems of cloning are overcome. Already, they say, new cloning techniques are being developed. For instance, scientists announced on April 27, 2000, that they had produced six cows by cloning in which the telomeres were much longer than in normal cows.[5] And some researchers feel that cloning will produce no more defects than normal births because it bypasses the most common form of birth defects, having the wrong number of chromosomes. With cloning, one begins with a healthy cell. According to some scientists, there is no compelling information proving that cloning is dangerous. But others cite the high rates of death and abnormalities in animal cloning experiments, and they point out that experiments with such risks are unacceptable in humans.

WHY CLONE A PERSON?

Even if cloning humans became possible, why would anyone want to clone a human? Some people envision special circumstances in which it might be acceptable, or even desirable, to clone humans, but not everyone agrees. Following are some of the circumstances under which people imagine cloning might take place.

To replace a child who has died. If cloning were possible, some parents, especially those who were unable to produce more children, might consider replacing a dead child with a clone of itself. Conceivably, this could be done if some of the dead child's tissue were collected just before or right after death. The collected tissue could be used to produce a child that would bear a strong physical resemblance to the dead child, its genetic parent. It is unlikely, though, that the cloned child would have the same personality. While genetics plays an important part in establishing who we are, our personalities are also shaped by our life's experiences.

As an alternative to artificial insemination or in vitro fertilization. On January 26, 2001, Panos Zavos, of the University of Kentucky, and Serverino Antinori, an Italian fertility doctor, announced plans to launch a serious project to clone humans to provide children for infertile couples. Working along with other international reproductive experts, they expect a cloned embryo to be the beginning of a baby that will be born in the next year or two.[6]

For some couples unable to conceive a child naturally, cloning might be an answer. Such couples might prefer creating a clone of themselves to accepting donor eggs or sperm from a third party. This option might have particular appeal to lesbian couples who want children.[7]

To save lives. Each year thousands of sick or injured people are saved through tissue and organ transplants. Yet thousands of others die because compatible organs or tissue cannot be obtained. Conceivably, cloning a sick or injured person could give rise to an individual who could provide the needed tissue or organ.

While the idea of cloning a person for the sole purpose of harvesting tissue or an organ from that person sounds far-fetched, precedents have already been established. No one knows how many children have been conceived as prospective donors. Some women get pregnant and have the fetus tested to see if it's a match for an ailing child. If the unborn child cannot serve as a donor, it might be aborted and the couple might try again.

Adam Nash was the first baby to be born after genetic testing of his embryo showed that he would have the traits necessary to provide a cell transplant for his dying six-year-old sister. Adam's parents chose in vitro fertilization, in which their sperm and eggs were joined in the laboratory. When the embryos reached the blastocyst stage, one cell was removed and tested to make certain it had the genetic qualities to make it compatible for the transplant. The genetic testing also showed that the chosen embryo did not carry his sister's disease, Fanconi anemia, that often leads to leukemia.

Adam was born on August 29, 2000, and soon afterward his sister received blood from the umbilical cord that connected him with the placenta in his mother's uterus. This stem cell-rich blood was expected to create a new immune system and blood supply for his sister. This experimental procedure appeared to work.

Not every child who needs a transplant can receive one from cord blood of a sibling or a relative who matches tissue type, but a cloned sibling would definitely provide a match for tissue and organ transplants. This idea seems ghoulish to some, but Lori Andrews, an expert on legal issues of reproduction, was told by a doctor that if any of his relatives got cancer, he would not hesitate to clone them and use the clones to provide organs to save their lives.[8]

To re-create extraordinary people. Each generation produces individuals who are extraordinarily gifted in some way—an Einstein, a Mozart, or a Gandhi, for instance. Some people suggest that society would benefit if individuals of such great talent were cloned. Although the idea is intriguing, scientists point out that there would be no assurance that a clone of an extraordinary individual would develop the same capabilities and talents. After all, a person is the sum of genetics, upbringing, and environment.

To create a master race. The idea of creating a master race of superstrong or superintelligent people has been around for a long time. Adolf Hitler, for instance, planned to create a master race by killing off groups he considered inferior and encouraging groups he considered superior to propagate.[9] Are there other Hitler types in the world who would view cloning as a way of producing a master race? If cloning were to become a viable method of producing human offspring, some people fear that a dictator might use cloning to form races of terrorists or warriors. But again this is probably a far-fetched fear. There would be no guarantee that a clone of a terrorist would become a terrorist.

THE ETHICS OF CLONING

The theoretical possibility of creating from one to hundreds of genetically identical humans has been called creepy, scary, revolting, immoral, and exciting. Would clones understand themselves as creations or just copies? Would cloning undermine the conception of a human being's individuality?

Many professionals and laymen believe that people should never be cloned, but others feel that human cloning is an important part of medicine's brave new world.

Religious leaders express widely different views about cloning. The Catholic moral tradition views the cloning of a human being as "a violation of human dignity," because it tampers with human life. From an Islamic standpoint, it is morally and religiously wrong to employ cloning technology for purposes other than therapeutic. Saving a life without destroying another does not seem wrong. However, Buddhists find no real philosophical problem with cloning. They believe that there is no such thing as two identical, existent beings and that genetic makeup is only an outer physical manifestation of the person. The mind is always fresh and unique. Cloning to benefit others is considered quite different from cloning to become rich and famous, so motivation is the important factor for Buddhists.

According to Moshe Tendler, an Orthodox Jewish rabbi, people knew what was good and what was evil in most areas of life until cloning became a possibility. Now, he feels, we are not so sure what is good and what is evil: "Cloning may not be intrinsically good or evil. The question really is will applications of cloning be a transgression by humans into the domain of God?"

Some religious leaders ask, "Can you clone a soul?" If each human consists of a material body animated by an immaterial personal self, what happens if many replicas of a body are made? Is it possible that a unique soul would inhabit each of the identical bodies? On would it be soulless?

Lee M. Silver, author of *Remaking Eden,* lectures widely on the social impact of biotechnology. He points out that no one questions the souls or individuality of identical twins. Cloning would not necessarily give rise to children who are as loving, talented, intelligent, or ethical as the person from whom they were cloned, but they would be unique individuals with their own memories and consciousness. They could be good or bad.

Committees of different religious leaders continue to debate the morality of cloning. Most suggest that cloning is an idea that should be put on hold. Nancy Duff, a theologian at the Princeton Theological Seminary, is quoted as saying, "Many people wonder if this [cloning] is a miracle for which we can thank God, or an ominous new way to play God ourselves."

Some who oppose the idea of cloning do so for consideration of the child created from such a procedure. Suppose the child were cloned to replace a child that had died? How would a child cloned to replace another feel? How would the parents, consciously or unconsciously, treat the

WHAT IF...
A BRAVE NEW WORLD NIGHTMARE

THE YEAR IS 2100. SARAH IS A TECHNICIAN WHO DRAWS BLOOD FOR MEDICAL TESTS AT A LARGE CLINIC. WHEN SHE SEES THAT A FAMOUS ATHLETE IS ON HER LIST OF PATIENTS FOR THE DAY, SHE HATCHES A SCHEME WITH A FRIEND WHO WORKS IN A NEARBY FERTILITY CLINIC.

AFTER DRAWING THE BLOOD FROM THE ATHLETE, SARAH USES A PIPETTE TO TRANSFER A SMALL PORTION INTO A TINY TUBE THAT SHE HAS HIDDEN IN HER POCKETBOOK. TEN MINUTES LATER, SHE LEAVES WORK AND TAKES THE STOLEN BLOOD TO HER FRIEND. THE FRIEND TRANSFERS THE BLOOD TO A LABORATORY DISH, WHERE IT IS NOURISHED AND TREATED WITH CHEMICALS THAT CAUSE IT TO PRODUCE MILLIONS OF IDENTICAL CELLS. MANY OF THESE CELLS HAVE A NUCLEUS WITH THE GENES OF THE ATHLETE.

THE WOMEN FREEZE THE CELLS. THEN THEY SELL THEIR CONTRABAND ON THE BLACK MARKET TO PEOPLE WHO WANT A CLONE OF THE ATHLETE.[10]

IS SUCH A SCENARIO POSSIBLE? IF POSSIBLE, IS IT LIKELY THERE WOULD EVER BE A MARKET FOR CELEBRITY CLONES? IT'S AN INTRIGUING QUESTION. IF CLONING BECAME COMMONPLACE, THERE WOULD CERTAINLY BE PLENTY OF OPPORTUNITIES FOR UNSCRUPULOUS PEOPLE TO COLLECT TISSUE SAMPLES FROM CELEBRITIES WITHOUT THEIR BEING AWARE OF IT. AFTER ALL, ONE LEAVES SKIN AT THE MANICURIST, BLOOD AT THE MEDICAL LABORATORY, AND SCALP CELLS AT THE HAIRDRESSER.

child if he or she did not measure up to the precious child who died?

Or suppose a child were brought into this world to provide tissue and organs for its genetic parent? Might the child lack self-worth? And would the person who received the organ or tissue transplant feel forever beholden to its clone? And suppose the cloned child became alienated from the parents or refused to cooperate in case an organ was needed. Would the child be loved as much as children who were born for other reasons?

While many ethicists feel that cloning should be put on hold until more is known about it, others point out that the genie is out of the bottle and say that cloning cannot be stopped. They want to develop safeguards to prevent abuse. Most reasons for cloning a person are frowned on by doctors and the general public. The impulse to create genetic copies of deceased loved ones or of oneself or one's heroes has been described as shallow and perhaps disgusting.[11] But many experts fear that laws that forbid cloning will drive it underground where there will be less control than if it were legal.

In January 2001, the British Parliament legalized therapeutic cloning. The scientists who created Dolly are in favor of this limited kind of cloning which involves early-stage embryos. Such embryos would not be planted in a uterus, and would not become babies. Rather they would be reprogrammed to produce only certain types of cells, embryonic stem cells. These cells would be grown in the lab to make replacement body cells for treating diseases such as Parkinson's. They would be of the patient's own genetic type, thus minimizing rejection. This is cloning for medical purposes, but there are questions about whether or not therapeutic cloning to develop spare parts will lead to whole body cloning.[12]

RESPECT FOR ALL LIFE

The debate over the ethics of cloning adds fodder to another debate—the ethics of using fertilized eggs or fetal tissue for scientific and medical purposes. Currently, some people argue that life begins at the moment of conception and therefore a fertilized egg should be valued as a living human being. These people object to any use of fertilized eggs or fetal tissue for scientific or medical purposes. But with cloning, the nucleus of almost any cell in the adult body could be regarded as equivalent to a fertilized egg. It is genetically complete and could, with human assistance, begin the process of development toward birth. How much this observation affects prevailing reasoning about the respect due to fertilized eggs, embryos, and our bodies in general remains to be seen.

To some, this new understanding puts into question the idea that a fertilized egg or a fetus, for that matter, is any more sacred than any other cell. While respecting those who consider all life sacred, Dr. Wilmut suggests a contrasting view. According to Wilmut, the embryo is merely a cluster of cells that does not become sentient until much later in development.

In spite of laws against experiments on human cloning and strong objections from scientists and the public, someone, somewhere will succeed in cloning a human.

Chapter Seven
EXPLORING GENES

News Flash! Scientists have just discovered the recipe for YOU! Human Genome Project leaders announced on June 26, 2000, that they finished sequencing almost all the human genome—the three billion nucleotide bases that form the chain of DNA inside almost every human cell. After spending millions of dollars and years of research, scientists are finished—for now. That is, scientists have finished one more step in the ongoing pursuit of information about human genetics, the science of heredity. This milestone, compared by some with man's landing on the moon, is hailed as one of the greatest achievements in the history of mankind.

Assembling the complete code of human DNA marks the end of an enormously long and difficult research project that took more than a decade of constant effort by many scientists using revolutionary technology. And it was based on knowledge accumulated by many other geneticists in the years before it even started.

Geneticists have come a long way since Gregor Mendel initiated the first experiments to study genetics.

Through years of patient work with pea plants in his monastery garden in the nineteenth century, Mendel observed and described the basic laws of heredity. He described "factors," which later became known as genes, that produced various outward traits in his subjects, such as color or size. Later scientists built on Mendel's experiments and discoveries to learn more about heredity and genetics.

In 1905, both Nettie Stevens and Edmund Beecher Wilson, working independently, discovered that sex is determined by the X and Y chromosomes. Scientists conducted experiments on fruit flies, bread mold, pea plants, mice, corn, E. coli, and many other organisms. They discovered tiny threadlike chromosomes in cells that contain the genes.

In 1910, Thomas Hunt Morgan produced the first chromosome map, showing the location of genes, but it was not known until 1944 that genes are made mostly of the molecule DNA (deoxyribonucleic acid). In 1953, James Watson and Francis Crick, aided by the work of Rosalind Franklin, who took X-ray photographs of DNA, revealed the shape and structure of the DNA molecule, the now famous double helix. In 1960, RNA (ribonucleic acid) was found to be the messenger that carries the genetic message from DNA to the cell's protein-making factories. These scientists discovered the "blueprint for human life," but they still did not understand it completely.

In the years that followed, scientists began to commercialize their knowledge of DNA. In 1976 the first genetic engineering company, Genentech, began to make medicines using information about genes and how they work. Researchers finally discovered oncogenes, genes linked to cancer in humans. In 1983, James Gusella demonstrated that the gene for Huntington's disease is on Chromosome 4. Yet scientists still did not know enough about genes and DNA to develop safe, reliable treatments for genetic diseases like some cancers and Huntington's disease.

THE HUMAN GENOME PROJECT

The Human Genome Project began in 1990 to fill in the gaps of our genetic knowledge and hopefully to bring scientists closer to finding cures for genetic diseases. Its main goal was to map all human genes and the stretches of DNA on chromosomes between them that contain no genes. The project was international in scope. At least eighteen countries established human genome research projects.

The U.S. Department of Energy and the National Institutes of Health together with major universities make up the United States genome program. In 1998 maverick scientist Craig Venter formed a privately financed company, Celera Genomics Corporation of Rockville, Maryland, to enter the

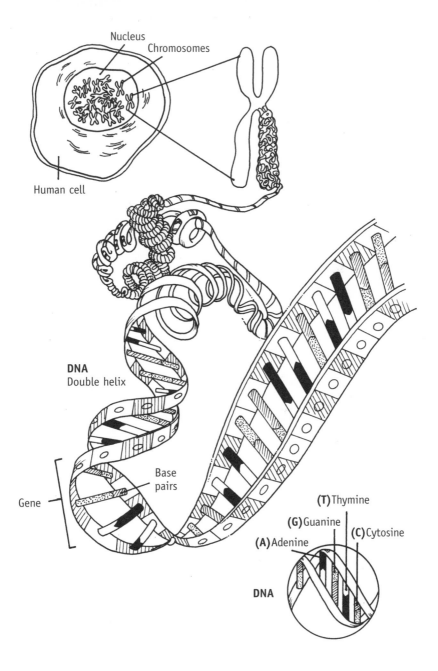

Nucleus

Chromosomes

Human cell

DNA
Double helix

Gene

Base
pairs

(T) Thymine

(G) Guanine

(A) Adenine

(C) Cytosine

DNA

The Human Genome Project involves sequencing the human genome—
the three billion nucleotide bases that form the chain of DNA inside
almost every human cell.

competition. Celera's entry in the project sped up the rate at which work was done.

In December 1999, a team of U.S. scientists announced that they had reached a major milestone. They had decoded the genetic instructions for an entire human chromosome, Chromosome 22. This chromosome contains genes related to some thirty diseases, including cancer and mental retardation. Then on June 26, 2000, Celera and the Human Genome Project announced that they had completed the first draft of the complete human genome, including all 23 pairs of chromosomes. By February 2001 both groups reported their first analysis of their data.

Both the number of genes themselves and the amount of new data about them are mind-boggling. No one can really imagine the scope of these human genome projects. They have piled up mountains of data.[1] Consider the following: If the DNA sequence of the human genome were compiled in books, the equivalent of 200 volumes the size of a Manhattan telephone book (1,000 pages each) would be needed to hold it. It would take a person about nine and a half years to read aloud (without stopping) the three billion bases in one's genome sequence, based on a rate of ten bases per second.[2]

Many people ask whose genome was chosen for mapping. Actually, samples from different individuals are being used in the project, so when the total project is finished it will not be the genome for any one individual. Instead, it will be a general map of humankind as a whole.

NEXT STEP

Decoding a whole chromosome means greater speed in tracking down genes that affect many diseases. The next step for genome project researchers is to identify the role of each gene. Knowing where each trait can be found will allow doctors to test for specific diseases using DNA testing. Knowing where to find a genetic defect is the first step in being able to repair that defect.

While the genome project is expected to bring a revolution in predicting and preventing disease, this may not happen as fast as many believe it will.[3] Needless to say, the process of determining the exact sequence of bases in DNA is an extremely complicated task. Actual genes that code for proteins and go wrong in cancer and genetic diseases occupy less than 3 percent of the total. The rest of the genes in the genome are called genetic noise.[4]

Changes in genes, mutations, occur in everyone, but many mutations produce no obvious effect.[5] Each of us carries about a half dozen defective genes. Most do no harm, but in some cases, just one mutant gene, one that is not normal, can

97

A GENETIC PRIMER

GENES HAVE BEEN CALLED THE SINGLE MOST IMPORTANT FACTOR THAT DISTINGUISHES ONE PERSON FROM ANOTHER. YOUR EYE COLOR, HAIR COLOR, AND OTHER PHYSICAL CHARACTERISTICS ARE DETERMINED BY THE GENES YOU INHERIT. MANY BEHAVIORS, SUCH AS RISK-TAKING AND SHYNESS, APPEAR TO BE PARTLY DETERMINED BY GENES.

GENES ARE PIECES OF DNA, OR DEOXYRIBONUCLEIC ACID, A MOLECULE THAT IS MADE OF JUST FOUR DIFFERENT BUILDING BLOCKS, OR NUCLEOTIDE BASES. THE HUMAN SCRIPT IS STORED IN A LANGUAGE OF FOUR LETTERS, COMMONLY KNOWN AS A (ADENINE), T (THYMINE), C (CYTOSINE), AND G (GUANINE). LONG STRANDS OF THESE NUCLEOTIDE BASES ARE PAIRED TOGETHER WITH ADENINE LINKED TO THYMINE AND GUANINE LINKED TO CYTOSINE. THE TWO RIBBONLIKE STRANDS WRAP AROUND EACH OTHER, FORMING A DNA MOLECULE RESEMBLING A TWISTED LADDER THAT IS CALLED A DOUBLE HELIX. THE RUNGS ON THE LADDER ARE MADE OF CHEMICAL BASES. THE DOUBLE HELIX OF DNA IS NOW A FAMILIAR SIGHT.

THE ARRANGEMENT OF BASES IS DIFFERENT IN EACH GENE AND MEANS DIFFERENT THINGS, MUCH AS THE LETTERS IN THE WORD "STAR" MEAN SOMETHING DIFFERENT WHEN THEY ARE ARRANGED AS "RATS." THERE ARE THOUSANDS OR MILLIONS OF BASES IN A SINGLE GENE, SOMEWHAT LIKE A WORD WITH MILLIONS OF LETTERS. THERE CAN BE A HUGE NUMBER OF COMBINATIONS.[6]

DNA IS COILED INTO TIGHTLY TWISTED PACKETS CALLED CHROMOSOMES. THERE ARE 46 HUMAN CHROMOSOMES (23 PAIRS)

IN ALMOST EVERY CELL IN THE HUMAN BODY AND THEY HOUSE 3
BILLION BASE PAIRS OF DNA THAT MAKE ABOUT 30,000 OR
MORE GENES.

THESE GENES CONTAIN THE INSTRUCTIONS FOR MAKING
500,000 TO A MILLION KINDS OF PROTEINS, THE
CHEMICALS THAT MAKE UP THE CELLS OF THE BODY AND DIRECT
THEIR ACTIVITIES. ONE KIND CARRIES THE OXYGEN IN YOUR
BLOOD; OTHER KINDS, ALONE OR IN COMBINATION, DIRECT OR
REGULATE EVERY FUNCTION IN YOUR BODY. IF ALL THE DNA
STRANDS IN A TINY SINGLE CELL WERE STRETCHED OUT AND TIED
TOGETHER AT THE ENDS, THEY WOULD BE ABOUT 5 FEET (1.5
METERS) LONG AND ONLY 50 TRILLIONTHS OF AN INCH WIDE.[7]

ALTHOUGH PEOPLE DIFFER WIDELY, THEIR DNA IS
MOSTLY THE SAME. YOU HAVE 99.9 PERCENT THE SAME DNA AS
JULIA ROBERTS, TOM CRUISE, ALBERT EINSTEIN, FLORENCE
NIGHTINGALE, ADOLF HITLER, BOB DYLAN, AND EVERYONE ELSE,
BUT THE NUMBER OF GENES IS SO HUGE THAT THE ONE-TENTH
OF 1 PERCENT THAT IS NOT THE SAME CAN MAKE A BIG
DIFFERENCE. IN FACT, ONE-TENTH OF 1 PERCENT MEANS
ROUGHLY 3 MILLION DIFFERENCES BETWEEN TWO INDIVIDUALS,
AND THESE DIFFERENCES ARE RESPONSIBLE FOR ALL THE
INHERITED VARIATIONS AMONG PEOPLE. EVEN IDENTICAL
TWINS WHO HAVE THE SAME DNA SCRIPT HAVE MANY
INDIVIDUAL DIFFERENCES.

result in a serious disease, such as Huntington's disease, cystic fibrosis, or sickle-cell anemia. In many diseases, a combination of genes is involved, but in each case, it is only a very small amount of DNA that is abnormal.

Defects within a cell's DNA are also involved in illnesses such as cancer, heart disease, psychiatric illness, and diabetes.[8] Although the genetic basis of such diseases may be so complex that gene therapy is impossible, scientists hope to develop new treatments by studying genes. Information about genes is expected to become the nucleus of future medicine.[9]

BIOLOGY'S MOONSHOT OR JUST HOOPLA?

Technology and resources based on mapping genes already have had profound impacts on biomedical research and clinical medicine.[10] Increasingly detailed maps have aided researchers seeking genes associated with dozens of conditions, including a kind of inherited colon cancer, Alzheimer's disease, and familial breast cancer. Improvements in disease diagnosis and prediction, curing diseases through replacing genes, and developing better drugs are just some of the goals of the Human Genome Project.

This project is expected to reap fantastic benefits, some of which can be anticipated and others that will be surprises. Nonetheless, not all scientists embrace the project.

The fact that the genetic code is being studied as a collage of humanity detracts from its value, says Roger Shattuck, a well-respected author and scholar. He and other critics of the Human Genome Project feel that the project is good science gone bad; that it has deluded us into false hopes. According to Shattuck, concentration on one aspect of life, the blindly mechanical genes, distracts us from the proper understanding of ourselves. And it upsets the balance of federally funded scientific investigation. Perhaps most disappointment about the Human Genome Project will come from the pace at which new medicines and methods of disease prevention appear. Many cures may be years in the future, rather than tomorrow, as many media predictions imply.[11]

The future will have serious ethical, social, and legal complications. Who should have access to personal genetic information and how will it be used? Will the use of genetic information by insurers, employers, courts, schools, adoption agencies, and the military be fair? If information is not kept confidential, even a bank might obtain information about whether or not a person's future health could prevent repayment of a loan. Many other societal concerns arise from the new genetics, such as the way to counsel parents about the risks and limitations of genetic technology. Personal genetic information can affect society's perception of an individual.

An individual may feel stigmatized because of genetic inheritance. More knowledge about the connection between behavior and genes may have a strong influence on the treatment of problems such as violence and drug abuse.

The effect of the new biology on ethical, legal, and social issues could be huge. The United States has devoted from 3 to 5 percent of the budget for its Human Genome Project to these issues. They are expected to become even more important as the genomic age progresses. Today is just the beginning.

Madison was desperately worried when her sister developed breast cancer. She, of course, was concerned about her sister's welfare and did everything she could to support her through her treatment. But she was also worried about herself. Her mother had died of cancer that spread from her breasts to other organs, and both her grandmothers had breast cancer. Madison insisted on being tested for the breast cancer genes. Laboratory technicians compared the DNA in some of her white blood cells with normal DNA. When the results came back, Madison learned that she did indeed have a gene for breast cancer. But then what to do? Doctors told Madison that she had several options.

Madison could take the drastic step of having both breasts removed to protect her from getting the disease. The removal of both breasts of high-risk women when they are still healthy usually prevents cancer from occurring, but it is a drastic, perhaps unnecessary, action. According to the American Cancer Society, about 25 percent of women diagnosed at age thirty-five or earlier are believed to carry the breast cancer gene BRCA1 or BRCA2, yet only 5 to 10 percent of patients who get breast cancer have a family history of the cancer.

There are less drastic ways of dealing with a high risk of breast cancer. Madison's tests showed only that she was "cancer prone," not that she would definitely get the disease. Careful monthly self-examinations, low-fat diet, exercise, and avoidance of estrogen were an alternative to the more drastic measure of removing her two healthy breasts.

Madison chose to keep her breasts and follow her doctor's advice to take all the possible steps to avoid cancer. She also agreed to get regular checkups to make certain that if she did develop cancer it would be caught at an early stage. The tests that indicated she carried a gene for breast cancer could eventually save her life by acting as a warning system.

GENE TESTS

Today, gene tests are available for a number of cancers and other diseases. These include Lou Gehrig's disease (progressive loss of motor function leading to paralysis and death), Gaucher's disease (enlarged liver and spleen, bone degeneration), Charcot-Marie-Tooth disease (loss of feeling in ends of limbs),

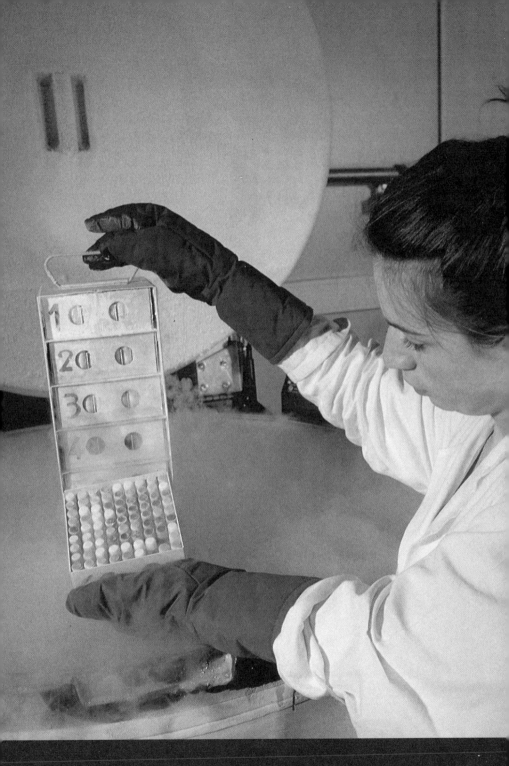

A scientist records a family illness at a DNA bank. Studying human genes can help determine whether a person is likely to develop certain genetic disorders.

dystonia (muscle rigidity, repetitive twisting movements), hemophilia A and B (bleeding disorders), sickle-cell disease (blood cell disorder, chronic pain, and infections), spinal muscular atrophy (severe, usually lethal, progressive muscle-wasting disorder in children), and Tay-Sachs disease (fatal neurological disease of early childhood, seizures, paralysis).

Already gene testing has dramatically improved the lives of many people who are at high risk for a number of disorders. For instance, aggressive monitoring for and the removal of growths in the colon in people inheriting a gene for a type of colon cancer can prevent fatalities. Scientists believe that in the future gene testing will become common-place. By the time your grandchildren go to the doctor, rapid and more specific tests will be based on a person's own geneprint, a record of the genes in a person's body. This will make prevention and earlier treatment of diseases possible.

GENE TESTING TOMORROW

Your granddaughter, baby Emily, is visiting the pediatrician for the first time. He flicks a cotton swab into her mouth and collects a sample of mucus from inside her cheek. While the doctor is examining Emily, a nurse takes the sample on the swab to the laboratory in the next office and compares her

A doctor and a counselor help a couple decide whether or
not to undergo gene testing.

genes against a computerized genome. The printer records
Emily's genes and labels the abnormal ones.

Now, the pediatrician can use this information to
prevent problems that might come up when Emily is older. For
example, one of her genes indicates that she is predisposed to
cardiovascular disease. The pediatrician suggests limiting the
amount of fat in Emily's diet beginning when she is two years
old. This, and other sensible measures, may prevent heart
disease from developing. Genetic testing may also predict if
Emily will benefit from, or be allergic to, different medications.

PERSONALIZED DRUGS

Gene testing can be used to tailor drug treatments to fit each patient. Today, doctors may prescribe one drug, find it does not help very much, then try another until they find the drug that works best with their patient. Since each person is different, it is not surprising that certain drugs work better on some people than on others.

In the future, doctors will be able to consult a patient's genetic profile to determine which type of medicine is most likely needed. With the use of information from the genome, new drugs will be made that are safer, more powerful, and more selective than ever before.[1]

In another twenty years, a person who has cancer of the uterus may go to her doctor's office and have him take a few cells from her tumor and place them on a microchip. Within minutes, the chip will be compared with a chip with a normal genome and the mutant genes that pushed the tumor to grow will be identified. Then new drugs may directly target the gene that is not normal.

In addition to the use of personalized drugs to treat tumors, a drug may be tailored to prevent the side effects that the patient might have experienced before the days of genetic profiles. Some researchers are already applying genetic data to existing drugs to screen out people most likely to have side effects from them. Before prescribing a drug, a doctor can screen a person's genetic profile against the profiles of patients who have had bad reactions to it and thus find out if that person should take or avoid the drug. For example, about 3 percent of the people who take an experimental drug for asthma develop liver abnormalities. If patients who are considered for the drug are screened to see if their genetic profiles are similar to those of people who suffer the abnormality, they can avoid the drug, if necessary.

Knowledge about sections of DNA segments called SNPs (pronounced "snips") plays an important part in personalizing drugs. The full name for SNPs is single nucleotide polymorphisms. SNPs are variations in the genetic code that occur about every one thousand bases along the three billion bases of the human genome. Special chips coated with DNA strands that are normal can be compared with chips containing SNPs of an individual, and drugs can be made based on this comparison. The number of personalized drug prescriptions is expected to increase dramatically when it costs less to identify SNPs. Knowledge about SNPs is predicted to make a quantum leap toward patient-specific medicine.

GENE THERAPY

According to the March of Dimes, gene therapy may be the best weapon ever brought to the fight against birth defects and many other health problems.[2] More than 390 gene therapy studies were performed on more than 4,000 patients in the last decade, according to the National Institutes of Health. Thirty years from now, essentially every disease will have gene-based therapy as a treatment option.[3]

GENE THERAPY

In gene therapy, a defective gene is replaced with a normal one.

❶ A healthy gene is inserted into the genetic structure of a virus.

❷ Altered viruses are injected into defective cells and link up with the DNA.

❸ The genetically corrected cells proliferate and displace cells with the defective gene.

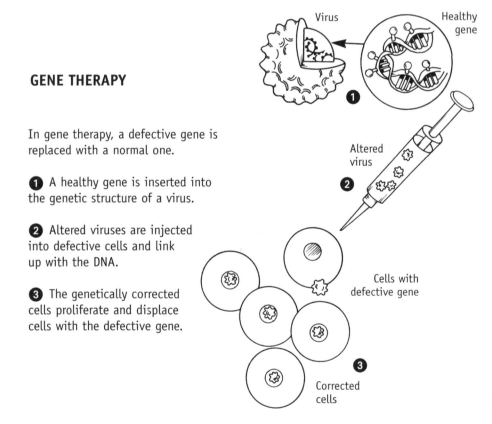

Virus

Healthy gene

❶

Altered virus

❷

Cells with defective gene

Corrected cells

❸

In this promising new therapy, a bad gene is replaced with a good one. Take the case of Ashanti. She was born in 1986 with an inherited disorder known as ADA (adenosine deaminase) deficiency. Every germ to which she was exposed made her sick because her immune system was defective. She was given a drug to protect her, but, although it worked well for some children with her condition, it did little for Ashanti. She was chosen to be the first person to receive medically approved gene therapy.

In 1990, a team of researchers extracted certain cells known as T cells from the immune system in Ashanti's blood and exposed them to viruses in which human ADA genes had been spliced. These viruses carried the ADA gene with them when they were returned to her body through blood dripped into her veins. The viruses carrying the gene invaded her T cells and inserted the healthy gene. This therapy was repeated a number of times during the next two years, and it corrected the disorder. At the age of thirteen, Ashanti was living a normal life, but she was not considered completely cured. She was still taking medicine regularly to make certain her disease does not recur.[4]

Since Ashanti's experimental procedure, similar clinical trials are being evaluated for many different diseases. Gene therapy can be used to slow down the production of excess cholesterol in the blood, an inherited disease. But getting the new gene into the body where it will replace the defective one is a difficult challenge.

In many experiments viruses are used as carriers, or vectors, because they naturally cause infections by invading a cell and inserting DNA into the nucleus. Scientists take advantage of the virus's natural tendency to integrate DNA with its host cell. To insert a gene into a virus, a scientist uses enzymes to take out the virus's disease-causing gene and insert the new healthy human gene. The patient is then "infected" with the modified virus, which is supposed to integrate with the person's own DNA. But this procedure is quite complicated, and there are many problems.

Nevertheless, new discoveries are helping doctors to reach their goal of correcting disorders and curing diseases by gene therapy. In experiments at the University of Pennsylvania's Institute for Human Gene Therapy, some patients with cystic fibrosis have received an altered virus directly into their lungs in the form of a fine aerosol from a novel spraying device. This places normal genes where they are most needed.[5]

Another approach is to insert a gene directly into a muscle, such as the heart, where it is needed to replace defective DNA. As an alternative to surgery, doctors can inject genetically engineered DNA that triggers the growth of blood vessels directly into a person's heart muscle. At St. Elizabeth's Medical Center in Boston, doctors found that heart muscle cells then produce a naturally occurring human protein that stimulates the growth of new vessels in the blood-starved area of the heart. In other words, the body grows its own coronary vessel bypass without surgery.[6]

HOPE FOR HUNTINGTON'S DISEASE

Consider what genetic medicine can mean to a person like Tyler. He is brilliant, athletic, handsome, and popular, but at the age of forty he is beginning to show symptoms of a fatal disease caused by a defect in a single gene. He is developing Huntington's disease, a progressive disorder of the brain that leads to loss of memory and other intellectual functions, uncontrollable movements, and emotional problems.

Scientists know that Tyler and others with Huntington's disease have an abnormality in a gene called ITI5. The search to identify this gene took ten years and nobody yet knows how it causes the disease.[7] Soon, however, doctors hope to be able to replace the gene that causes Tyler's disease with a normal one. And someday, they may be able to change his genes so that the disease cannot be passed on to his children.

AN EXPERIMENT BRINGS CAUTION

The sudden death of Jesse Gelisinger, a patient undergoing gene therapy in an experimental procedure for which he volunteered, was a setback for gene therapy. Gelisinger was suffering from a liver disorder, and the experiment, if successful, was to help babies born with a severe form of the disease. On September 13, 1999, a high dose of adenovirus, a common cold virus that is used to put good genes into people's bodies, was pumped into his blood. Four days after that, he died. Later, it was concluded that Gelisinger should not have been included in the study because his liver was not functioning well enough. His death was a wake-up call for more care in the monitoring of the selection of patients in clinical trials and in the entire experimental procedure. Since that time, stricter guidelines have been put in place for trial procedures.

A SUCCESS STORY

After years of dashed hopes, scientists in France announced the first completely successful use of gene therapy on April 27, 2000. The doctors treated three babies who had the rare immune disorder SCID, severe combined immunodeficiency. This disease is caused by a defect in a gene that is needed to make T cells. In some cases, bone marrow transplants can be used to treat the disease, but if this treatment does not work, patients must be protected from infection by living in germ-free bubbles. Partial success with gene therapy had been achieved in the case of Ashanti, mentioned earlier, but since she had to continue taking medicine, it was not considered a complete success. But the French procedure had unequivocally succeeded.[8] Two of the babies were healthy a year later, and the procedure was continued with good results for other babies suffering from the same condition.

GERMLINE THERAPY

Gene therapy cures the patient but does not protect the patient's offspring. Germline therapy is therapy that could prevent hereditary diseases from being passed from one generation to the next. In germline therapy mutant genes are replaced by normal ones in the reproductive cells known as germ cells. Germ cells divide to form egg and sperm, which also carry the normal gene. The normal gene is passed on to the person's offspring with the egg or sperm cell, so the child does not carry the defective gene or develop the disease.

Scientists are not yet experimenting with germline therapy in humans, but this therapy is being widely used for the production of transgenic animals, animals of combined species, for research and agriculture.

Early in 2001, scientists at the Oregon Regional Primate Research Center announced the arrival of ANDi, a monkey with the gene of another animal in his cells. ANDi, whose name is a backward acronym for "inserted DNA", began life as an unfertilized egg in which a gene from a jellyfish had been inserted. His development followed much the same procedure as that of a test-tube baby.

ANDi's birth caused great excitement among scientists, for this was the first primate on which germline therapy had been attempted. Traces of the jellyfish gene were detected in ANDi's muscle, blood cells, hair, and cheek. When ANDi sexually matures at the age of four or five, scientists will learn whether or not his sperm carry the gene.

The birth of ANDi is a step toward producing monkeys with human genes. Such animals could be powerful tools for studying and eventually curing many human diseases. Animal rights activists and others, however, are critical of this use of a primate for medical purposes. Ethicists, such as Arthur Caplan of the University of Pennsylvania Medical Center and Jeffrey

Kahn of the University of Minnesota, called for establishing policies to deal with genetic manipulation now, before it goes too far.[9]

Because of its potential for abuse, germline therapy in humans needs to be widely discussed and evaluated. As far back as 1998, a team of prestigious scientists and bioethicists announced that with germline therapy humankind would have the power to direct its own evolution within two or three decades.[10] To some ethicists, this is a frightening concept.

In addition, many scientists warn that there will be tremendous risks involved. The Council for Responsible Genetics warns that germline therapy could go horribly wrong in unexpected ways and that mistakes could show up generations later. Or an offspring's genes may be changed in ways not planned.[11] But for those close to someone who is suffering from a terrible disease, germline therapy, if it becomes available, may seem worth the risk.

Consider Brandon, a boy who suffers from Lesch-Nyhan syndrome, and his parents. This is a rare but horrible genetically transmitted disease in which the body fails to produce a particular enzyme, the lack of which leads to bizarre behavior. Brandon has episodes in which he bites chunks out of his lips, tongue, fingers, and other parts of his flesh. He pleads for restraints when he feels this violent, self-destructive behavior approaching, and his family do all they can to help him. But there is no cure.

While gene therapy for Lesch-Nyhan syndrome is in the experimental stage, gene therapy is not an option for Brandon at this point. If germline therapy were to become available, members of his family who have witnessed his suffering might consider it to make sure their future offspring do not suffer from this dreadful disease.

ETHICAL CONSIDERATIONS

Despite its promise, the new genetics carries serious risks as well as benefits. With the ability to use genes to predict and treat disease comes the ability to use them for purposes beyond therapy.

Genetic testing opens a brave new world with a host of ethical and legal questions. Will it lead to invasions of privacy? Will results of tests be used by insurance companies or employers to identify and reject people with risks? Will a doctor be vulnerable to a malpractice suit if he or she gives information based on a faulty test?

Germline therapy raises other questions. According to a survey sponsored by the National Center for Genome Resources, a majority of Americans approve of germline therapy, the kind of gene therapy that would prevent disease in a person's descendants.[12] Many religious leaders also support experiments in germline therapy. Even the Catholic Church, which is usually conservative in these areas, supports germline therapy with some reservations.[13] Its potential to prevent human suffering is awesome. But germline therapy could just as easily be used to produce designer babies—offspring with desirable characteristics such as beautiful features, long legs, or large breasts. Would this be appropriate?

Germline gene therapy involves more than the patient, the family, and the doctor—it involves all the generations to come. Society has a stake in determining how germline therapy is to be used. Critics warn that tinkering with the human gene pool could have consequences we cannot foresee.[14]

The tremendous benefits and the problems that ensue with new advances in genetic medicine will continue for years to come. In December 1999, IBM announced a five-year project, Blue Gene, that will feed genetic data into a supercomputer to help researchers understand basic biological processes. The new supercomputer is expected to be five hundred times more powerful than the supercomputers in operation in 1999. But nature is so complex that it will take the computer a year to accomplish its task.[15] Such comparisons help us to appreciate the complexity of living things.

Chapter Nine
STAYING HUMAN IN MEDICINE'S BRAVE NEW WORLD

Where is medicine's brave new world taking us? Advances come so rapidly that they often occur in uncharted legal and ethical waters. Along with awesome benefits, will there be negative consequences?

The human body still holds many mysteries. High-tech babies bring joy to many parents who might never have had children, but for some childless couples nothing can be done. For others, there are too many babies at one time. Some parents are pushed into a thicket of ethical problems. How far should research go in assisting reproduction?

Cloning once seemed like science fiction, but many believe it is not a question of whether or not it will happen but when. Therapeutic cloning has been legalized in Britain. Research that could lay the groundwork for human cloning is proceeding rapidly. Many people find the idea of cloning a human disgusting. Would you change your mind if a relative's life could be saved by the cloning of organs? Suppose a clone enters your social world. How would you feel? If you object to cloning, do you want to make it illegal?

Researchers are hard at work trying to mend spinal cords. Everyone supports this effort, but the use of spare parts of different animals in human beings is a subject of controversy. Might we reach the point where we are no longer human if many spare parts come from other kinds of animals? Suppose the use of a part from another kind of animal could help a paralyzed person to walk again. If you accept using a pig valve to mend your heart, do you accept the transplant of genes from one animal to another to aid in the prevention and cure of disease?

Artificial organ supplies and whole organs from stem cells are already beginning to do away with the science fiction nightmare in which human parts are supplied by a headless frozen clone. Stem cell research uses biological building blocks, the ancestral cells for all tissues. Charles Krauthammer believes the debate over fetal tissue overlooks the big issue. While some people are upset about the destruction of potential human embryos that may later be destroyed at the reproductive centers where they are stored, others are asking where the study of these cells is taking us? Is the logical by-product of medicine's brave new world hybrid human-animal species, partly developed bodies for use as spare parts?[1]

Genes have been identified that appear to influence behavior such as risk taking, sexual preference, and intelligence.

The genes that influence body size and muscle mass are known. With such knowledge many characteristics of a baby can be determined even before an embryo is placed in a woman's uterus. Genetic determination can help to prevent disease and to provide offspring who can help to cure siblings, but suppose it leads to experiments to produce children with characteristics that are not health related. If scientists begin to see humans as a product of manufacture, they could cross a line that may be irreversible. Will genetic engineering be used to change characteristics for cosmetic purposes such as hair loss? Where might the reengineering of humans end?

For some individuals, tinkering with the genes of the human body represents the ultimate nightmare. Will medicine's brave new world lead to the end of evolutionary pressures that have shaped humanity? Or is the ability of humans to manage their own evolution one that distinguishes them from every other species?

Critics continue to ask if tinkering with the human gene pool will have consequences we cannot foresee.[2] Will the benefits of the revolution in medicine and biology be extended to all people throughout the world regardless of their nationality or economic condition? Or will the new biology lead to the creation of an exclusive set of strong, healthy, wealthy, and beautiful people living in rich countries, a super-tribe or master

Scientists study bands of DNA, or DNA fingerprints, using a technique called electrophoresis. DNA testing can help prove whether two people are related, whether a child carries the gene for a genetic disease, or whether a suspect committed a crime.

race of the sort dreamed of by the Nazis and feared by the rest of the world?

In the coming decades, new frontiers in medicine will shape social, political, and moral debates. Everyone understands the importance of medical research, but those who remember that humankind's essential nature is more than DNA must help shape these debates.[3] They can draw the line at the use of genetic engineering for inappropriate purposes and support groups whose role will be to define and maintain the ethics of new technologies in medicine.

You, too, can get involved. Some magazines and Web sites conduct polls on subjects where you may vote by expressing an opinion online. The National Institutes of Health occasionally asks for input on certain subjects. You can find this by checking the news at www.nih.gov. In addition, some chat groups offer a chance for serious discussion of biotechnology, while others encourage the opinions of laymen who have no background in the subject. Serious citizens need to be selective in this area.

You can help to see that medicine's brave new world will be a better world in which health is greatly improved and the qualities that make us human are protected, valued, and extolled. You can be an informed citizen. You live in exciting times.

adult stem cells: also called multipotent. Specialized cells that develop from embryonic stem cells. Found in children and adults.

angiogenesis: the creation of new blood vessels.

artificial insemination: the injection of semen into a woman's uterus (not through sexual intercourse) in order to make her pregnant.

bases: chemical ingredients of genes, rungs on the ladder of DNA.

biotechnology: the use of biological techniques to produce new products for industry and medicine.

blastocyst: a stage in the development of an embryo. A hollow sphere that forms after an egg is fertilized.

chromosomes: strands of genetic material contained in the nucleus of a cell. Each chromosome consists of one very long strand of DNA, folded and coiled to produce a compact body.

clone: an organism that is genetically identical to another.

DNA (deoxyribonucleic acid): material inside the nucleus of a cell that carries genetic information.

embryo: the developing human from about two weeks to three months after conception.

embryonic stem cells: cells found in the pre-embryo within four to seven days after fertilization. Includes totipotent and pluripotent stem cells.

genes: basic units of heredity that direct almost every aspect of the construction, operation, and repair of living organisms. Almost every human cell has 30,000 or more genes arranged like beads on a string (chromosome). Each gene is a set of biochemical instructions that tells a cell how to assemble one of many proteins. Each protein carries out its own highly specialized role.

gene therapy: the insertion of normal or altered genes into cells to overcome the function of missing or defective genes.

genetic engineering: the science of rearranging DNA molecules to modify the expression of a gene. Used in people, plants, and animals to correct disease and improve characteristics.

genome: the sum of all the DNA in an organism.

germ cells: cells that divide to form the male and female reproductive cells, the sperm and eggs.

germline therapy: the altering of genes in germ cells. Changes will be carried from one generation to the next because egg and sperm cells contain genes identical to those in germ cells.

in vitro fertilization: mixing of eggs with sperm in the laboratory to achieve conception.

mesenchymal stem cells: adult stem cells that can give rise to bone, cartilage, tendons, fat, and muscle cells.

multipotent stem cells: *see* adult stem cells.

mutation: a change in the string of DNA that makes up a gene. A mutant gene that no longer codes for the proper protein can cause a genetic disease.

nuclear transfer: a process in which DNA is removed from an unfertilized egg and the nucleus of a body cell from another individual is introduced. Then the combination is fused to begin development.

pluripotent stem cells: *see* embryonic stem cells.

proteins: the basic chemicals that make up the structure of cells and direct their activities.

SCNT somatic cell: a body cell not involved in reproduction.

SNPs (single nucleotide polymorphisms): variations in DNA that occur in about every one thousand bases.

stem cells: cells that have the ability to divide without limits and give rise to different kinds of cells in the human body. Ancestral cells for all the body's tissue.

tissue engineering: a way of building new tissue by replicating cells.

totipotent stem cell: the single cell, or zygote, that is formed when an egg is fertilized by a sperm.

transgenic: an organism with genes from more than one species.

xenotransplant: an organ or tissue removed from an individual of one species and transplanted into an individual of another species. For example, many people have received heart valves from pigs.

zygote: see totipotent stem cell.

Notes

To OUR READERS: All the Internet addresses in this book were active and correct when the book went to press.

Chapter One

1. www.intelihealth.com/IH/ihtIH?t=333&st+333&r=EMIHC000&c=220573
2. Bryan Appleyard, *Brave New Worlds: Staying Human in the Genetic Future* (New York: Viking, 1998), p. 42.
3. "Mining the Genome," *Technology Review*, September/October 1999, p. 58.
4. "The Biotech Century," *Time*, January 11, 1999, p. 43

Chapter Two

1. "New Ways to Help Sperm Get Up and Go," *New York Times*, February 17, 1999.
2. Gina Kolata, *Clone: The Road to Dolly and the Path Ahead* (New York: William Morrow, 1998), pp. 10–11.
3. "Just Another Girl," *New York Times*, October 27, 1999.
4. "In Vitro Fertilization (IVF)," Microsoft Encarta Encyclopedia Online 2000.
5. "Mothers with Another's Eggs," *U.S. News & World Report*, April 12, 1999, p. 42.
6. www.asrm.org/current/press/fetalegg.html
7. "How to Coax New Life," Special Issue, *Time*, Fall 1996, p. 37.
8. www.asrm.org/current/press/fetalegg.html
9. www.asrm.org/Media/Ethics/fetalegg.html
10. http://dailynews.yahoo.com/h/nm/20000427/sc/healthfertility_2.html
11. Lee Silver, *Remaking Eden* (New York: Avon Books, 1998), pp. 303–304.
12. "Dancer Gets First Ovarian-Tissue Transplant," *Science News*, October 2, 1999, p. 212.
13. "The Sperminator," *New York Times Magazine*, March 25, 1999, p. 64.
14. Bruno Leone, ed., *Biomedical Ethics: Opposing Viewpoints* (San Diego, CA: Greenhaven Press, 1998), p. 109.
15. "As Octuplets Remain in Peril, Ethics Questions Are Raised," *New York Times*, December 22, 1998.
16. "As Octuplets Remain in Peril."

17. "On Web, Models Auction Their Eggs to Bidders for Beautiful Children," *New York Times*, October 23, 1999.

Chapter Three
1. "Repairing the Damaged Spinal Cord," *Scientific American*, September 1999, pp. 67–68.
2. "To Stand and Raise a Glass," *Newsweek*, July 1, 1996, p. 53.
3. Rachel Engers, "Navigating the Spinal Cord," *Yale Medicine*, Winter/Spring 1998, Feature Story.
4. "No Dullard; Spinal Cord Proves It Can Learn," *New York Times*, September 21, 1999.
5. John W. McDonald and the Research Consortium of the Christopher Reeve Paralysis Foundation, "Repairing the Damaged Spinal Cord," *Scientific American*, September 1999, p. 70.
6. "Surgical Procedure Offers Hope Against Spina Bifida," *Intelihealth*, October 28, 1999.
7. www.sbaa.org/html/sbaa_facts.html
8. www.spinal-research.org/news_room.htm
9. www.intelihealth.com/IH/ihtIH/EMIHC000/333/333/266325.html
10. www.intelihealth.com/IH/ihtIH/EMIHC000/333/333/266325.html
11. www.wired.com/news/print_version/technolgy/medtech/story/20000.html
12. Robert J. White, "Head Transplants," *Scientific American Presents*, September 1999, p. 24.

Chapter Four
1. www.unos.org.
2. Sandra Blaluslee, "On Watch for Any Hint of Mad Cow Disease," *New York Times*, January 30, 2001.
3. BBC News Online: Despatches, "Animal Organ Transplant Patient Seeks to Allay Fears." http://news.bbc.co.uk/lo/english/despatches/newsid_56000/56787.stm
4. R.P. Lanza, D.K.C. Cooper, and W.L. Chick, "Xenotransplantation," *Scientific American*, July 1997, p. 54.
5. M. Wortman, "Once the Stuff of Myth and Science Fiction, the Transgenic Mouse, First Created at Yale, Has Conquered the World of Biomedicine," *Yale Medicine*, Fall 1999–Winter 2000. p. 27.
6. S.G. Stolberg, "Could This Pig Save Your Life?" *New York Times Magazine*, October 3, 1999, pp. 46–51.
7. C. Cowley, "A Pig May Someday Save Your Life," *Newsweek*, January 1, 2000. p. 88.

8. L. Altman, "Drug Agency Proposes New Guidelines on Animal Transplants," *New York Times*, September 21, 1996, p.10.
9. Peter Gorner, "Pig Organs Appear Fit for Human Transplant," *Chicago Tribune*, August 20, 1999.
10. K. Paradis, et al., "Search for Cross-Species Transmission of Porcine Endogenous Retroviruses in Patients Treated with Living Pig Tissue," *Science* 285 (1999), pp. 1236–1241.
11. Leonard Bell, M.D., personal communication, January 13, 2000.
12. www.alexionpharm.com./techplat/unigraft.cfm
13. R.A. Knox, "Pig Cell Transplant for Parkinson's," *Boston Globe*, www.nytsyn.com/live/Elderly/063_030497_160004_18348.html.
14. C. Arnst and J. Carey, "Biotech Bodies," *Business Week*, July 27, 1998, p. 56.
15. D.J. Mooney and A.G. Mikos, "Growing New Organs," *Scientific American*, April 1999, p. 60.
16. S. Hoerstrup, "A Trileaflet Heart Valve Grown in Vitro." Presented at the American Heart Association's 72nd Scientific Sessions, November 1999, Atlanta.
17. J. Cunningham, "Animal-to-Human Organ Transplants Could Save Lives," in B. Leone, ed., *Biomedical Ethics: Opposing Viewpoints* (San Diego: Greenhaven Press, 1998), p. 87.
18. W. J. Clinton, November 14, 1998, http://bioethics.gov/clinton_letter.html.
19. N. Wade, "Human Cells Revert to Embryo State, Scientists Assert," *New York Times*, November 12, 1998.
20. H.T. Shapiro, November 20, 1995, http://bioethics.gov/shapiro_letter.html.
21. D.C. Wertz, "Human Cells in Cows' Eggs: Another Source of Organs for Transplant," *Gene Letter* 3 (February 1999). www.geneletter.org/ 0299/cowseggs.htm

Chapter Five
1. www.nih.gov/news/stemcell/primer.htm
2. "Scientists Cultivate Cells from Which Human Life Is Created," *New York Times*, November 6, 1998.
3. www.nih.gov/news/stemcell/primer.htm
4. www.nih.gov/news/stemcell/primer.htm
5. www.intelihealth.com/IH/ihtIH?t=333&st=333&r=EMIHC000&c=228994
6. www.intelihealth.comIH/ihtIH?t=333&st=333&r=EMIHC000&c=204169

7. "The Hope and the Hype of Cord Blood," *New York Times*, December 1, 1998.
8. www.stemcellresearch.org/prentice.htm
9. http://ipn.intelihealth.com/...SIPN000/7187/7223/288131.htm?k=basePrint
10. www.unos.org
11. www.osirisistr.com/clinical/clinical_transplantation.htm
12. http://abcnews.go.com/sections/living/DailyNews/stemcells.html
13. "Embryonic Stem Cells for Medicine," *Scientific American*, April 1999, p. 71.
14. Robert J. White, "Do Human Embryos Have Rights?" *America*, June 19, 1999, p.7
15. www.stemcellresearch.org/nihresponse.htm

Chapter Six
1. Lee M. Silver, *Remaking Eden* (New York: Avon Books, 1998), p. 120
2. www.oregonlive.com/news/99/12/st121526.html
3. "What's Killing Clones?" *U.S. News & World Report*, May 24, 1999, p. 65.
4. "An Old Clone," *New York Times*, May 28, 1999.
5. www.cnn.com/2000/HEALTH/04/27/cloning.aging/index.html
6. Gina Kolata, "On Cloning Humans, 'Never' Turns Swiftly into 'Why Not,'" *New York Times*, December 2, 1997.
7. Ronald M. Green, *I, Clone* (New York: Scientific American Presents, 1999), p. 83.
8. Margaret Talbot, "A Desire to Duplicate," *New York Times Magazine*, February 4, 2001.
9. George B. Annas, Scientific Discoveries and Cloning: Challenges for Public Policy, testimony before the United States Senate, March 12, 1997.
10. Silver, pp. 145–146.
11. Martha Nussbaum and Cass R. Sunstein, eds., *Clones and Clones* (New York: W.W. Norton, 1998), p. 231.
12. http://news.bbc.co.uk/hi/english/sci/tech/newsid_710000/710445.stm
13. www.ornl.gov/hgmis/elsi/elsi/elsi.html

Chapter Seven
1. Antonio Regalado, "Mining the Genome," Technology Review, September-October 1999, p. 58.
2. www.ornl.gov/hgmis/faq/faqs1.html

3. John Carey, "Genes," Business Week, August 30, 1999, p. 153.
4. Regalado, p. 58.
5. "Mutations Galore," Scientific American, April 1999, p. 32.
6. Catherine Baker, Your Genes, Your Choices: Exploring Issues Raised by Genetic Research (Washington, D.C.: American Association for the Advancement of Science, 1997), p.16.
7. www.wnet.org/archive/innovation/show1/html/1sb-gene.html
8. www.mayohealth.org/9601/htm/genetics/htm
9. "One of 2 Teams in Genome Race Sets an Earlier Deadline," New York Times, March 16, 1999.
10. www.oml.gov/hgmis/publicat/97pr/02intro.html
11. Roger Shattuck, Forbidden Knowledge (New York: St. Martin's Press, 1996), pp. 221-223.

Chapter Eight

1. Christine Gorman, "Drugs by Design," Time, January 11, 1999, p. 80.
2. www.noah.cuny.e...genetics/genetics.html
3. W. French Anderson, "A Cure That May Cost Us Ourselves," Newsweek, January 1, 2000, p. 76.
4. "Ethical Issues in Human Gene Therapy," Human Genome News, 10: 1–2, February 1999, p. 1.
5. www.med.upenn.edu/ihgt/clintri/cf.html
6. www.intelihealth.com/IH/ihtInsider?t=2180&c=235223&r=EMIHC000
7. www.mayohealth.org/mayo/9512/htm/genetics.htm
8. Gina Kolata, "Scientists Report the First Success of Gene Therapy," New York Times, April 28, 2000.
9. Michael D. Hemrich, "Monkey Business," Time, January 22, 2001, pp. 40–42.
10. John Naisbitt, High Tech/High Touch: Technology and Our Search for Meaning (New York: Broadway Books/Random House, 1999), p. 123.
11. "Gene Therapy Results Surprise Scientists," Hartford Courant, November 15, 1999.
12. "Germ-line Gene Therapy Enters the Foreseeable Future," The Gene Letter, 3: 1 (August 1998), p. 1.
13. Naisbitt, p. 126.
14. Bryan Appleyard, Brave New Worlds: Staying Human in the Genetic Future (New York: Viking, 1998), p. 21.

15. "I.B.M. Plans a Supercomputer That Works at the Speed of Life," *New York Times*, December 6, 1999.

Chapter Nine
1. Charles Krauthammer, "Why Pro-Lifers Are Missing the Point," *Time*, February 12, 2001, p. 60.
2. Bryan Appleyard, *Brave New Worlds: Staying Human in the Genetic Future* (New York: Viking, 1998), p. 21.
3. "Looking Beyond Gene Maps," *Christian Science Monitor*, August 19, 1999.

Suggested Reading

Andrews, Lori. *The Clone Age: Adventures in the New World of Reproductive Technologies.* New York: Henry Holt, 1999.

Appleyard, Bryan. *Brave New Worlds: Staying Human in the Genetic Future.* New York: Viking, 1998.

Baker, Catherine. *Your Genes, Your Choices: Exploring Issues Raised by Genetic Research.* Washington, D.C.: American Association for the Advancement of Science, 1997.

Caplan, Arthur L., and Daniel H. Coelho, eds. *The Ethics of Organ Transplants: The Current Debate.* Amherst, NY: Prometheus Books, 1998.

Hamer, Dean, and Peter Copeland. *Living with Our Genes: Why They Matter More Than You Think.* New York: Doubleday, 1998.

Hyde, Margaret O., and Elizabeth H. Forsyth. *Medical Dilemmas.* New York: G.P. Putnam's Sons, 1990.

Hyde, Margaret, and John F. Setaro. *When the Brain Dies First.* Danbury, Conn.: Franklin Watts, 2000.

Kimbrell, Andrew. *The Human Body Shop: The Engineering and Marketing of Life.* Washington, D.C.: Regnery, 1998.

Kolata, Gina. *Clone: The Road to Dolly and The Path Ahead.* New York: William Morrow, 1998.

Marshal, Elizabeth. *Conquering Infertility.* Danbury, Conn.: Franklin Watts, 1997.

McGee, Glenn, ed. *The Human Cloning Debate*. Berkeley, Calif.: Berkeley Hills Books, 1998.

Naisbitt, John, with Nana Naisbitt and Douglas Philips. *High Tech/High Touch: Technology and Our Search for Meaning*. New York: Broadway Books, Random House, 1999.

Nussbaum, Marta C. and Cass R. Sunstien, eds. *Clones and Clones: Facts and Fantasies About Human Cloning*. New York: W.W. Norton, 1998.

Presnall, Judith. *Artificial Organs*. New York: Lucent Books, 1996.

Rainis, Kenneth, and George Nassis. *Biotechnology Projects for Young Scientists*. Danbury, Conn.: Franklin Watts, 1998.

Rantala, M.L., and Arthur Milgram, eds. *Cloning: For and Against*. Chicago: Open Court, 1999.

Reeve, Christopher. *Still Me*. New York: Random House, 1998.

Ridley, Matt. *Genome: The Autobiography of a Species in 23 Chapters*. New York: HarperCollins, 2000.

Roleff, Tamara, ed. *Biomedical Ethics: Opposing Viewpoints*. San Diego, CA: Greenhaven, 1998.

Rothblatt, Marine. *Unzipped Genes: Taking Charge of Baby-Making in the New Millennium*. Philadelphia: Temple University Press, 1997.

Silver, Lee M. *Remaking Eden: How Genetic Engineering and Cloning Will Transform the American Family*. New York: Avon Books, 1998.

Sherrow, Victoria. *Bioethics and High-Tech Medicine*. New York: Twenty-First Century Books, 1996.

Yount, Lisa. *Issues in Biomedical Ethics*. San Diego: Lucent Books, 1998.

For Further Information

American Society for Reproductive Medicine
(Formerly The American Fertility Society)
1209 Montgomery Highway
Birmingham, AL 35216
www.asrm.org
Patient education booklets

Christopher Reeve Paralysis Foundation
500 Morris Avenue
Springfield, NJ 07081
www.paralysis.org
Progress in research reports and news

The Hastings Center
Garrison, New York 10524
www.hastingscenter.org
Publishes books, papers, guidelines, and a bimonthly Hastings
Center Report

National Association of Surrogate Mothers
P.O. Box 1927
Oceanside, CA 92051
www.SurromomsOnline.com

National Bioethics Advisory Commission
6100 Executive Boulevard, Suite 5B01
Rockville, MD 20893
http://bioethics.gov

National Institute of Neurological Disorders and Stroke
National Institutes of Health

P.O. Box 5801
Bethesda, MD 20892
www.ninds.nih.gov
Sponsors an active public information program

National Multiple Sclerosis Society
733 Third Avenue, sixth floor
New York, NY 10017
http://www.nmss.org
Provides MS-related services and information

National Reference Center for Bioethics Literature
Kennedy Institute of Ethics
Georgetown University
www.georgetown.edu/research/nrcbl/nirehg.htm
800-633-3849
World's largest collection of material related to medical
ethics and biomedical research

Additional Related Online Sites

Dana Alliance for Brain Initiatives
www.dana.org
Programs, activities, and information about brain disease

EurekAlert
www.eurekalert.org
Comprehensive Web site about the latest research advances in science, medicine, health, and technology produced by the American Association for the Advancement of Science

Mayo Clinic's Health Oasis
www.mayohealth.org
General information

MedicineNet
www.medicinenet.com
Current medical news, treatment updates, and health facts

National Human Genome Research Institute
www.nhgri.nih.gov
Information about the Human Genome Project, including ethical, legal, and social implications

Neuroscience for Kids
http://faculty.washington.edu/chudler/newslet.html
Monthly newsletter about the brain, advances in medicine, and other valuable information

OnHealth
www.onhealth.com
More than 200 topics on health and daily briefings on health issues

Thrive
www.thriveonline.com
Information about various conditions, organizations, and hotlines for more than 100 organizations, plus access to MEDLINE for in-depth searching.

Index

defined, 77
ethics of, 85–91
human, 9, 79–91, 120
therapeutic, 89–90, 120
Colon cancer, 100, 106
Cord blood, 69, 84
Council for Responsible Genetics, 117
Cow eggs, 62–63
Creutzfeldt-Jakob disease, 47
Crick, Francis, 93
Cyst, 32
Cystic fibrosis, 100, 112
Cytosine, 98

Diabetes, 57–58
Dignity of life, 10
DNA (deoxyribonucleic acid), 52, 78, 92–94, *95*, 96–100, 103, *105*, 112, 113, 123
Dolly, *76*, 76–77, 79, 80
Donor eggs, 18–21, 23–24, 28, 29
Donor sperm, 23–24, 28
Dopamine, 56
Double helix, 93, *95*, 98
Duff, Nancy, 87
Dystonia, 106

Ebola virus, 47, 60
Electrophoresis, *123*
Embryonic stem cells, 65–67, 73–75, 90, 121
Energy, U.S. Department of, 94
Ethics, 10–12, 14, 62–63
cloning and, 85–91
donor sperm and eggs and, 29
germline therapy and, 116–117, 119
xenotransplantation and, 60–61

Fanconi anemia, 84
Fertility drugs, 26–28
Fetal tissue, 19, 21, 121

Folic acid, 39
Folkman, Judah, 59
Franklin, Rosalind, 93
Free radicals, 32

Gaucher's disease, 104
Gearhart, John D., 66
Gelisinger, Jesse, 114
Genentech, 94
Genes, 92–102, 121–122
Gene testing, 104, 105, 106–108, *107*, 118
Gene therapy, 10, 100, *110*, 110–115
Genetic databases, 11
Genetic engineering, 94, 112, 113
Genetic noise, 97
Genome (genetic profile), 10, 11
Germ cells, 115
Germline gene therapy, 115–119
Getty, Jeff, 48, 57
Glutamate, 32
Guanine, 98
Gusella, James, 94

Head transplants, 41–42
Heart transplants, 43, 45, 49, 50
Hemophilia A and B, 106
High-tech babies (*see* Assisted reproductive technologies)
Hitler, Adolf, 85
HIV/AIDS (human immunodeficiency virus), 47, 48, 54, 57, 60
Human brain transplants, 42
Human cloning, 9, 79–91, 120
Human Genome Project, 92, 94, *95*, 96–97, 100–102
Huntington's disease, 57, 94, 100, 113–114
Huxley, Aldous, 6–9, 11

IBM Corporation, 119
ICSI (intracytoplasmic sperm injection), 23

141